The Coronation by James Shirley

Previously attributed to John Fletcher.

James Shirley was born in London in September 1596.

His education was through a collection of England's finest establishments: Merchant Taylors' School, London, St John's College, Oxford, and St Catharine's College, Cambridge, where he took his B.A. degree in approximately 1618.

He first published in 1618, a poem entitled Echo, or the Unfortunate Lovers.

As with many artists of this period full details of his life and career are not recorded.

He wrote his first play, Love Tricks, or the School of Complement, which was licensed on February 10th, 1625.

For the next two decades, he would write prolifically and with great quality, across a spectrum of thirty plays; through tragedies and comedies to tragicomedies as well as several books of poetry. Unfortunately, his talents were left to wither when Parliament passed the Puritan edict in 1642, forbidding all stage plays and closing the theatres.

His death, at age seventy, along with that of his wife, in 1666, is described as one of fright and exposure due to the Great Fire of London which had raged through parts of London from September 2nd to the 5th.

He was buried at St Giles in the Fields, in London, on October 29th, 1666.

Index of Contents

DRAMATIS PERSONAE

Philocles
Lisander
Cassander
Lisimachus
Antigonu
Arcadius
Macarius
Seleucus
Queen
Charilla
Polidora
Nestorius
Eubulus
A Bishop
Poleanus
Sophia
Demetrius
Gentlemen and Gentlewomen
Servants and Attendants

PROLOGUE

Since 'tis become the Title of our Play,
A woman once in a Coronation may
With pardon, speak the Prologue, give as free
A welcome to the Theatre, as he
That with a little Beard, a long black Cloak,
With a starch'd face, and supple leg hath spoke
Before the Plays the twelvemonth, let me then
Present a welcome to these Gentlemen,
If you be kind, and noble, you will not
Think the worse of me for my Petticote:
But to the Play, the Poet bad me tell
His fears first in the Title, lest it swell
Some thoughts with expectation of a strain,
That but once could be seen in a Kings Reign,
This Coronation, he hopes you may
See often, while the genius of his Play,
Doth prophesie, the Conduits may run Wine,
When the days triumph's ended, and divine
Brisk Nectar swell his Temples to a rage,
With something of more price t' invest the Stage.

There rests but to prepare you, that although
It be a Coronation, there doth flow
No undermirth, such as doth lard the Scene
For course delight the language here is clean.
And confident, our Poet bade me say,
He'll bate you but the folly of a Play.
For which, although dull souls his Pen despise,
Who thinks it yet too early to be wise.
The nobler will thank his Muse, at least
Excuse him, cause his thought aim'd at the best,
But we conclude not, it does rest in you.
To censure Poet, Play, and Prologue too.
But what have I omitted? is there not
A blush upon my cheeks that I forgot
The Ladies, and a Female Prologue too?
Your pardon noble Gentlewomen, you
Were first within my thoughts, I know you sit
As free, and high Commissioners of wit,
Have clear, and active souls, nay, though the men
Were lost in your eyes, they'll be found agen,
You are the bright intelligences move,
And make a harmony this sphere of Love,
Be you propitious then, our Poet says,
Our wreath from you, is worth their grove of Bayes:

ACTUS PRIMUS

SCÆNA PRIMA

Enter **PHILOCLES** and **LISANDER**.

PHILOCLES
Make way for my Lord Protector.

LISANDER
Your graces servants.

[Enter **CASSANDER**, and **LISIMACHUS**.

CASSANDER
I like your diligent waiting, where's Lisimachus?

LISIMACHUS
I wait upon you, Sir.

CASSANDER

The Queen looks pleasant
This morning, does she not?

LISIMACHUS
I ever found
Her gracious smiles on me.

CASSANDER
She does consult
Her safety in't, for I must tell thee boy,
But in the assurance of her love to thee,
I should advance thy hopes another way,
And use the power I have in Epire, to
Settle our own, and uncontrouled greatness;
But since she carries her self so fairly,
I am content to expect, and by her marriage
Secure thy fortune, that's all my ambition
Now, be still careful in thy applications
To her, I must attend other affairs,
Return, and use what Art thou canst to lay
More charms of love upon her.

LISIMACHUS
I presume
She always speaks the language of her heart,
And I can be ambitious for no more
Happiness on earth, than she encourages
Me to expect.

CASSANDER
It was an act becoming
The wisdom of her Father to engage
A tye between our Families, and she
Hath play'd her best discretion to allow it;
But we lose time in conference, wait on her,
And be what thou wert born for, King of Epire,
I must away.

[Exit.

LISIMACHUS
Success ever attend you.
Is not the Queen yet coming forth?

LISANDER
Your servant,
You may command our duties,
This is the Court Star, Philocles.

PHILOCLES
The Star that we must sail by.

LISANDER
All must borrow
A light from him, the young Queen directs all
Her favours that way.

PHILOCLES
He's a noble Gentleman,
And worthy of his expectations:
Too good to be the son of such a Father.

LISANDER
Peace, remember he is Lord Protector.

PHILOCLES
We have more need of Heavens Protection
I' th' mean time, I wonder the old King
Did in his life, design him for the office.

LISANDER
He might expect his faith, I have heard when
The King, who was no Epirote, advanc'd
His claim, Cassander, our Protector now,
Young then, oppos'd him toughly with his faction,
But forc'd to yield, had fair conditions,
And was declar'd by the whole State, next heir;
If the King wanted issue, our hopes only
Thriv'd in this daughter.

PHILOCLES
Whom but for her smiles
And hope of marriage with Lisimachus,
His Father, by some cunning, had remov'd
E'r this.

LISANDER
Take heed, the Arras may have ears
I should not weep much if his grace would hence
Remove to Heaven.

PHILOCLES
I prethee what should he do there?

LISANDER
Some Offices will fall.

PHILOCLES
And the Skie too, e'r I get one stair higher
While he's in place.

[Enter **ANTIGONUS**.

ANTIGONUS
Lisander, Philocles,
How looks the day upon us? where's the Queen?

PHILOCLES
In her bed-chamber.

ANTIGONUS
Who was with her?

LISANDER
None but the young Lord Lisimachus.

ANTIGONUS
'Tis no treason
If a man wish himself a Courtier
Of such a possibility: he has
The mounting fate.

PHILOCLES
I would his Father were
Mounted to th' gallows.

ANTIGONUS
He has a path fair enough,
If he survive by title of his Father.

LISANDER
The Queen will hasten his ascent.

PHILOCLES
Would I were Queen.

ANTIGONUS
Thou wou'dst become rarely the petticoat,
What wou'dst thou do?

PHILOCLES
Why, I wou'd marry
My Gentleman usher, and trust all the strength
And burden of my State upon his legs,

Rather than be call'd wife by any son
Of such a Father.

LISANDER
Come, let's leave this subject,
We may find more secure discourse; when saw
You young Arcadius, Lord Macarius's Nephew?

ANTIGONUS
There's a spark, a youth moulded for a Favourite,
The Queen might do him honor.

PHILOCLES
Favourite, 'tis too cheap a name, there were a match
Now for her Virgin blood.

LISANDER
Must every man
That has a handsome face or leg, feed such
Ambition: I confess I honor him,
He has a nimble soul, and gives great hope
To be no woman-hater, dances handsomly,
Can court a Lady powerfully, but more goes
To th' making of a Prince. He's here
And's Uncle.

[Enter **ARCADIUS**, **MARCARIUS**, **SELEUCUS**.

SELEUCUS
Save you Gentlemen, who can direct me
To find my Lord Protector?

LISANDER
He was here
Within this half hour, young Lisimachus
His Son is with the Queen.

SELEUCUS
There let him compliment,
I have other business, ha, Arcadius!

[Exit.

PHILOCLES
Observ'd you, with what eyes Arcadius
And he saluted, their two families
Will hardly reconcile.

ANTIGONUS
Seleucus carries
Himself too roughly; with what pride and scorn
He past by 'em.

LISANDER
Th'other with less shew
Of anger, carries pride enough in's soul,
I wish 'em all at peace, Macarius looks
Are without civil war, a good old man,
The old King lov'd him well, Seleucus Father
Was as dear to him, and maintain'd the character
Of an honest Lord through Epire: that two men
So lov'd of others, should be so unwelcome
To one another.

ARCADIUS
The Queen was not wont to send for me.

MACARIUS
The reason's to her self,
It will become your duty to attend her.

ARCADIUS
Save you Gentlemen, what novelty
Does the Court breathe to day?

LISANDER
None Sir, the news
That took the last impression is, that you
Purpose to leave the Kingdom, and those men,
That honor you, take no delight to hear it.

ARCADIUS
I have ambition to see the difference
Of Courts, and this may spare; the delights
At home do surfet, and the Mistriss, whom
We all do serve, is fixt upon one object,
Her beams are too much pointed, but no Countrey
Shall make me lose your memories.

[Enter **QUEEN, LISIMACHUS, MACARIUS, CHARILLA.**

QUEEN
Arcadius.

MACARIUS
Your Lordship honor'd me,

I have no blessing in his absence.

LISIMACHUS
'Tis done like a pious Uncle.

QUEEN
We must not
Give any licence.

ARCADIUS
If your Majesty
Would please.

QUEEN
We are not pleas'd, it had become your duty,
To have first acquainted us, e'r you declar'd
Your resolution publick, is our Court
Not worth your stay?

ARCADIUS
I humbly beg your pardon.

QUEEN
Where's Lysimachus?

LISIMACHUS
Your humble servant, Madam.

QUEEN
We shall find
Employment at home for you, do not lose us.

ARCADIUS
Madam, I then write my self blest on earth
When I may do you service.

QUEEN
We would be private, Macarius.

MACARIUS
Madam, you have blest me,
Nothing but your command could interpose to
Stay him.

QUEEN
Lisimachus,
You must not leave us.

LISANDER
Nothing but Lisimachus? has she not
Ta'en a philter?

QUEEN
Nay, pray be cover'd, Ceremony from you,
Must be excus'd.

LISIMACHUS
It will become my duty.

QUEEN
Not your love?
I know you would not have me look upon
Your person as a Courtier, not as Favorite;
That Title were too narrow to express
How we esteem you.

LISIMACHUS
The least of all
These names from you, Madam, is grace enough.

QUEEN
Yet here you wou'd not rest?

LISIMACHUS
Not if you please:
To say there is a happiness beyond,
And teach my ambition how to make it mine,
Although the honors you already have
Let fall upon your servant, exceed all
My merit; I have a heart is studious
To reach it with desert, and make if possible
Your favor's mine by justice, with your pardon.

QUEEN
We are confident this needs no pardon, Sir,
But a reward to cherish your opinion,
And that you may keep warm your passion,
Know we resolve for marriage, and if
I had another gift, beside my self,
Greater, in that you should discern, how much
My heart is fixt.

LISIMACHUS
Let me digest my blessing.

QUEEN

But I cannot resolve when this shall be.

LISIMACHUS
How Madam? do not make me dream of Heaven,
And wake me into misery, if your purpose
Be, to immortalize your humble servant,
Your power on earth's divine, Princes are here
The copies of Eternity, and create,
When they but will our happiness.

QUEEN
I shall
Believe you mock me in this argument,
I have no power.

LISIMACHUS
How, no power?

QUEEN
Not as a Queen.

LISIMACHUS
I understand you not.

QUEEN
I must obey, your Father's my Protector.

LISIMACHUS
How?

QUEEN
When I am absolute, Lisimachus,
Our power and Titles meet, before, we are but
A shadow, and to give you that were nothing.

LISIMACHUS
Excellent Queen,
My love took no original from State,
Or the desire of other greatness,
Above what my birth may challenge modestly,
I love your virtues; mercenary souls
Are taken with advancement, you've an Empire
Within you, better than the worlds, to that
Looks my ambition.

QUEEN
T'other is not, Sir,
To be despis'd, Cosmography allows

Epire, a place i' th' Map, and know till I
Possess what I was born to, and alone
Do grasp the Kingdoms Scepter, I account
My self divided, he that marries me
Shall take an absolute Queen to his warm bosom,
My temples yet are naked, until then
Our Loves can be but compliments, and wishes,
Yet very hearty ones.

LISIMACHUS
I apprehend.

QUEEN
Your Father.

[Enter **CASSANDER** and **SELEUCUS**.

CASSANDER
Madam, a Gentleman has an humble suit.

QUEEN
'Tis in your power to grant, you are Protector,
I am not yet a Queen.

CASSANDER
How's this?

LISIMACHUS
I shall expound her meaning.

QUEEN
Why kneel you, Sir?

SELEUCUS
Madam, to reconcile two families
That may unite, both Counsels and their blood
To serve your Crown.

QUEEN
Macarius, and Eubulus
That beare inveterate malice to each other.
It grew, as I have heard, upon the question
Which some of either family had made
Which of their Fathers was the best Commander:
If we believe our stories, they have both
Deserved well of our state, and yet this quarrel
Has cost too many lives, a severe faction.

SELEUCUS
But I'll propound a way to plant a quiet
And peace in both our houses, which are torn
With their dissentions, and lose the glory
Of their great names, my blood speaks my relation
To Eubulus, and I wish my veins were emptied
To appease their war.

QUEEN
Thou hast a noble soul,
This is a charity above thy youth,
And it flows bravely from thee, name the way.

SELEUCUS
In such a desperate cause, a little stream
Of blood might purge the foulness of their hearts
If you'll prevent a deluge.

QUEEN
Be particular.

SELEUCUS
Let but your Majesty consent that two
May with their personal valour, undertake
The honor of their family, and determine
Their difference.

QUEEN
This rather will inlarge
Their hate, and be a means to call more blood
Into the stream.

SELEUCUS
Not if both families
Agree, and swear—

QUEEN
And who shall be the Champions?

SELEUCUS
I beg the honor, for Eubulus cause
To be ingag'd, if any for Macarius,
Worthy to wager heart with mine, accept it,
I am confident, Arcadius,
For honor would direct me to his sword,
Will not deny, to stake against my life
His own, if you vouchsafe us priviledge.

QUEEN
You are the expectation, and top boughs
Of both your houses, it would seem injustice,
To allow a civil war to cut you off,
And your selves the instruments, besides
You appear a soldier; Arcadius
Hath no acquaintance yet with rugged war,
More fit to drill a Lady, than expose
His body to such dangers: a small wound
I'th' head, may spoil the method of his hair,
Whose curiosity exacts more time,
Than his devotion, and who knows but he
May lose his ribond by it in his lock,
Dear as his Saint, with whom he would exchange
His head, for her gay colours; then his band
May be disorder'd, and transform'd from Lace
To Cutwork, his rich cloaths be discomplexioned
With bloud, beside the infashionable slashes:
And at the next Festival take Physick,
Or put on black, and mourn for his slain breeches:
His hands cas'd up in gloves all night, and sweet
Pomatum: the next day may be endanger'd
To blisters with a sword, how can he stand
Upon his guard, who hath Fidlers in his head,
To which, his feet must ever be a dancing?
Beside a falsify may spoil his cringe,
Or making of a leg, in which consists
Much of his Court-perfection.

SELEUCUS
Is this Character
Bestow'd on him?

QUEEN
It something may concern the Gentleman,
Whom if you please to challenge
To Dance, play on the Lute, or Sing.

SELEUCUS
Some catch?

QUEEN
He shall not want those will maintain him
For any sum.

SELEUCUS
You are my Sovereign,
I dare not think, yet I must speak somewhat,

I shall burst else, I have no skill in Jiggs,
Nor Tumbling.

QUEEN
How Sir?

SELEUCUS
Nor was I born a Minstrel, and in this you have
So infinitely disgrac'd Arcadius.
But that I have heard another Character,
And with your royal Licence do believe it,
I should not think him worth my killing.

QUEEN
Your killing?

SELEUCUS
Does she not jeer me;
I shall talk treason presently, I find it
At my tongues end already, this is an
Affront, I'll leave her.

QUEEN
Come back, do you know Arcadius?

SELEUCUS
I ha' chang'd but little breath with him; our persons
Admit no familiarity; we were
Born to live both at distance, yet I ha' seen him
Fight, and fight bravely.

QUEEN
When the spirit of Wine
Made his brain valiant, he fought bravely.

SELEUCUS
Although he be my enemy, should any
Of the gay flies that buzze about the Court,
Sit to catch trouts i'th' summer, tell me so,
I durst in any presence but your own.

QUEEN
What?

SELEUCUS
Tell him he were not honest.

QUEEN

I see Seleucus, thou art resolute,
And I but wrong'd Arcadius, your first
Request is granted, you shall fight, and he
That conquers be rewarded, to confirm
First place and honor to his Family:
Is it not this you plead for?

SELEUCUS
You are gracious.

QUEEN
Lisimachus.

LISIMACHUS
Madam.

CASSANDER
She has granted then?

SELEUCUS
With much ado.

CASSANDER
I wish thy sword may open
His wanton veins, Macarius is too popular,
And has taught him to insinuate.

QUEEN
It shall
But haste the confirmation of our loves,
And ripen the delights of marriage, Seleucus.

[Exit **SELEUCUS**.

LISIMACHUS
As I guest,
It cannot be too soon.

CASSANDER
To morrow then we crown her, and invest
My Son with Majesty, 'tis to my wishes,
Beget a race of Princes, my Lisimachus.

LISIMACHUS
First, let us marry, Sir.

CASSANDER
Thy brow was made

To wear a golden circle, I'm transported,
Thou shalt rule her, and I will govern thee.

LISIMACHUS
Although you be my Father, that will not
Concern my obedience, as I take it.

[Enter **PHILOCLES**, **LISANDER**, and **ANTIGONUS**.

Gentlemen,
Prepare your selves for a solemnity
Will turn the Kingdom into triumph, Epire
Look fresh to morrow, 'twill become your duties
In all your glory, to attend the Queen
At her Coronation, she is pleased to make
The next day happy in our Calendar,
My office doth expire, and my old blood
Renews with thought on't.

PHILOCLES
How's this?

ANTIGONUS
Crown'd to morrow.

LISANDER
And he so joyful to resign his Regency,
There's some trick in't, I do not like these hasty
Proceedings, and whirls of state, they have commonly
As strange and violent effects; well, heaven save the Queen.

PHILOCLES
Heaven save the Queen, say I, and send her a sprightly
Bed-fellow, for the Protector, let him pray for
Himself, he is like to have no benefit of my devotion.

CASSANDER
But this doth quicken my old heart, Lisimachus,
There is not any step into her throne,
But is the same degree of thy own state;
Come Gentlemen.

LISANDER
We attend your grace.

CASSANDER
Lisimachus.

LISIMACHUS
What heretofore could happen to mankind
Was with much pain to climb to heaven, but in
Sophias marriage of all Queens the best,
Heaven will come down to earth, to make me blest.

[Exeunt.

ACTUS SECUNDUS

SCÆNA PRIMA

Enter **ARCADIUS** and **POLIDORA**.

POLIDORA
Indeed you shall not go.

ARCADIUS
Whither?

POLIDORA
To travel,
I know you see me, but to take your leave,
But I must never yield to such an absence.

ARCADIUS
I prethee leave thy fears, I am commanded
To th' contrary, I wonot leave thee now.

POLIDORA
Commanded? by whom?

ARCADIUS
The Queen.

POLIDORA
I am very glad, for trust me, I could think
Of thy departure with no comfort, thou
Art all the joy I have, half of my soul,
But I must thank the Queen now for thy company,
I prethee, what could make thee so desirous
To be abroad?

ARCADIUS
Only to get an appetite
To thee Polidora.

POLIDORA
Then you must provoke it.

ARCADIUS
Nay, prethee do not so mistake thy servant.

POLIDORA
Perhaps you surfeit with my Love.

ARCADIUS
Thy love?

POLIDORA
Although I have no beauty to compare
With the best faces, I have a heart above
All competition.

ARCADIUS
Thou art jealous now,
Come let me take the kiss I gave thee last,
I am so confident of thee, no Lip
Has ravisht it from thine; I prethee come
To Court.

POLIDORA
For what?

ARCADIUS
There is the throne for beauty.

POLIDORA
'Tis safer dwelling here.

ARCADIUS
There's none will hurt,
Or dare but think an ill to Polidora,
The greatest will be proud to honor thee.
Thy luster wants the admiration here:
There thou wot shine indeed, and strike a reverence
Into the gazer.

POLIDORA
You can flatter too.

ARCADIUS
No praise of thee can be thought so, thy virtue
Will deserve all, I must confess, we Courtiers

Do oftentimes commend to shew our Art,
There is necessity sometimes to say,
This Madam breaths Arabian Gumms,
Amber and Cassia; though while we are praising,
We wish we had no nostrils to take in
Th' offensive steam of her corrupted Lungs.
Nay, some will swear they love their Mistriss,
Would hazard lives and fortunes, to preserve
One of her hairs brighter than Berinices;
Or young Apollo's, and yet after this,
A favour from another toy would tempt him
To laugh, while the officious hangman whips
Her head off.

POLIDORA
Fine men.

ARCADIUS
I am none of these,
Nay, there are women Polidora, too
That can do pretty well at flatteries;
Make men believe they dote, will languish for 'em,
Can kiss a Jewel out of one, and dally
A carcanet of Diamonds from another,
Weep into th' bosome, of a third, and make
Him drop as many Pearls; they count it nothing
To talk a reasonable heir within ten days
Out of his whole Estate, and make him mad
He has no more wealth to consume.

POLIDORA
You'll teach me
To think I may be flattered in your promises,
Since you live where this Art is most profest.

ARCADIUS
I dare not be so wicked Polidora,
The Infant errors of the Court I may
Be guilty of, but never to abuse
So rare a goodness, nor indeed did ever
Converse with any of those shames of Court,
To practise for base ends; be confident
My heart is full of thine, and I so deeply
Carry the figure of my Polidora,
It is not in the power of time or distance
To cancel it, by all that's blest I love thee:
Love thee above all women, dare invoke
A curse when I forsake thee.

POLIDORA
Let it be some
Gentle one.

ARCADIUS
Teach me an oath I prethee,
One strong enough to bind, if thou dost find
Any suspition of my faith, or else
Direct me in some horrid imprecation:
When I forsake thee for the love of other
Women, may heaven reward my apostacy
To blast my greatest happiness on earth,
And make all joys abortive.

POLIDORA
Revoke these hasty syllables, they carry
Too great a penalty for breach of Love
To me, I am not worth thy suffering,
You do not know, what beauty may invite
Your change, what happiness may tempt your eye
And heart together.

ARCADIUS
Should all the graces of your sex conspire
In one, and she should court me, with a Dowry,
Able to buy a Kingdom, when I give
My heart from Polidora.

POLIDORA
I suspect not,
And to requite thy constancy, I swear.

ARCADIUS
'Twere sin to let thee waste thy breath
I have assurance of thy noble thoughts.

[Enter a **SERVANT**.

SERVANT
My Lord, your Uncle hath been every where
I' th' Court inquiring for you, his looks speak
Some earnest cause.

ARCADIUS
I am more acquainted with
Thy virtue, than to imagine thou wilt not
Excuse me now, one kiss dismisses him

Whose heart shall wait on Polidora prethee
Let me not wish for thy return too often,
My Father.

[Enter **NESTORIUS**, and a **SERVANT**.

NESTORIUS
I met Arcadius in strange haste, he told me
He had been with thee.

POLIDORA
Some affair too soon
Ravish'd him hence, his Uncle sent for him
You came now from Court: how looks the Queen
This golden morning?

NESTORIUS
Like a Bride, her soul
Is all on mirth, her eyes have quick'ning fires,
Able to strike a spring into the earth,
In winter.

POLIDORA
Then Lisimachus can have
No frost in's blood, that lives so near her beams.

NESTORIUS
His politick Father the Protector smiles too,
Resolve to see the ceremony of the Queen
'Twill be a day of state.

POLIDORA
I am not well.

NESTORIUS
How! not well? retire then, I must return
My attendance is expected, Polidora,
Be careful of thy health.

POLIDORA
It will concern me.

[Exit.

[Enter **ARCADIUS**, and **MACARIUS**.

ARCADIUS
You amaze me, Sir.

MACARIUS

Dear Nephew, if thou respect thy safety
My honor, or my age, remove thy self,
Thy life's in danger.

ARCADIUS

Mine? who's my enemy?

MACARIUS

Take horse, and instantly forsake the City,
Or else within some unsuspected dwelling,
Obscure thy self, stay not to know the reason.

ARCADIUS

Sir, I beseech your pardon, which i' th' number
Of my offences unto any, should
Provoke this dishonourable flight?

MACARIUS

I would, when I petition'd for thy stay,
I had pleaded for thy banishment, thou knowst not
What threatens thee.

ARCADIUS

I would desire to know it,
I am in no conspiracy of treason,
Have ravish'd no mans Mistriss, not so much
As given the lye to any, what should mean
Your strange and violent fears, I will not stir
Until you make me sensible I have lost
My innocence.

MACARIUS

I must not live to see
Thy body full of wounds, it were less sin
To rip thy Fathers Marble, and fetch from
The reverend vault, his ashes, and disperse them
By some rude winds, where none should ever find
The sacred dust: it was his Legacy,
The breath he mingled with his prayers to Heaven
I should preserve Arcadius, whose fate
He prophesied in death, would need protection,
Thou wot disturb his ghost, and call it to
Affright my dreams, if thou refuse to obey me.

ARCADIUS

You more inflame me, to enquire the cause

Of your distraction, and you'll arm me better
Than any coward flight by acquainting me
Whose malice aims to kill me, good Sir tell me.

MACARIUS
Then prayers and tears assist me.

ARCADIUS
Sir.

MACARIUS
Arcadius,
Thou art a rash young man, witness the spirit
Of him that trusted me so much, I bleed,
Till I prevent this mischief.

[Exit.

[Enter **PHILOCLES**, **LISANDER**.

ARCADIUS
Ha, keep off.

PHILOCLES
What mean you, Sir?

LISIMACHUS
We are your friends.

ARCADIUS
I know your faces, but
Am not secure, I would not be betraid.

LISIMACHUS
You wrong our hearts, who truly honor you.

ARCADIUS
They say I must be kill'd.

PHILOCLES
By whom?

ARCADIUS
I know not, nor wou'd I part with life so tamely.

PHILOCLES
We dare engage ours in your quarrel, hide
Your sword, it may beget suspition,

It's enough to question you.

ARCADIUS
I am confident;
Pray pardon me, come, I despise all danger:
Yet a dear friend of mine, my Uncle told me
He would not see my body full of wounds.

LISIMACHUS
Your Uncle, this is strange.

ARCADIUS
Yes, my honest Uncle,
If my unlucky Stars have pointed me
So dire a fate.

PHILOCLES
There is some strange mistake in't.

[Enter **ANTIGONUS**.

ANTIGONUS
Arcadius, the Queen would speak with you,
You must make haste.

ARCADIUS
Though to my death, I flie
Upon her summons I give up my breath
Then willingly, if she command it from me.

PHILOCLES
This does a little trouble me.

LISIMACHUS
I know not
What to imagine, something is the ground
Of this perplexity, but I hope there is not
Any such danger as he apprehends.

[Enter **QUEEN, LISIMACHUS, MACARIUS, EUBULUS, SELEUCUS, ARCADIUS, LADIES, ATTENDANTS** and **GENTLEMAN**.

QUEEN
We have already granted to Seleucus
And they shall try their valour, if Arcadius
Have spirit in him to accept the challenge,
Our Royal word is past.

PHILOCLES
This is strange.

EUBULUS
Madam, my son knew not what he ask'd,
And you were cruel to consent so soon.

MACARIUS
Wherein have I offended, to be rob'd
At once, of all the wealth I have, Arcadius
Is part of me.

EUBULUS
Seleucus's life and mine
Are twisted on one thred, both stand or fall
Together, hath the service for my Countrey
Deserved but this reward, to be sent weeping
To my eternal home? Was't not enough
When I was young, to lose my bloud in wars,
But the poor remnant that is scarcely warm
And faintly creeping through my wither'd veins
Must be let out to make you sport.

MACARIUS
How can
We, that shall this morn see the sacred oyl,
Fall on your Virgin tresses, hope for any
Protection hereafter, when this day
You sacrifice the blood of them that pray for you.
Arcadius, I prethee speak thy self,
It is for thee I plead.

EUBULUS
Seleucus, kneel
And say thou hast repented thy rash suit;
If e'er I see thee fight, I be thus wounded,
How will the least drop forc'd from thy veins,
Afflict my heart.

MACARIUS
Why, that's good;
Arcadius, speak to her; hear him Madam.

ARCADIUS
If you call back this honor you have done me
I shall repent I live, doe not perswade me:
Seleucus, thou art a noble enemy,
And I will love thy soul, though I despair

Our bodies friendly conversation:
I would we were to tugg upon some cliffe,
Or like two prodigies i'th' air, our conflict
Might generally be gaz'd at, and our bloud
Appease our grandsires ashes.

MACARIUS
I am undone.

SELEUCUS
Madam, my father says I have offended,
If so, I beg your pardon, but beseech you
For your own glory, call not back your word.

EUBULUS
They are both mad.

QUEEN
No more, we have resolv'd,
And since their courage is so nobly flam'd,
This morning we'll behold the Champions
Within the List, be not afraid, their strife
Will stretch so far as death, so soon as we
Are Crown'd, prepare your selves, Seleucus.

[Kisses her hand.

SELEUCUS
I have receiv'd another life in this high favour,
And may lose what nature gave me.

QUEEN
Arcadius, to encourage thy young valour,
We give thee our Fathers sword.
Command it from our Armory; Lisimachus,
To our Coronation.

[Exeunt.

SELEUCUS
I'll forfeit
My head for a rebellion, than suffer it.

[Exit.

ARCADIUS
I am circled with confusions, I'll do somewhat
My brains and friends assist me.

[Exit.

PHILOCLES
But do you think they'll fight indeed?

LISIMACHUS
Perhaps
Her Majesty will see a bout or two.
And yet 'tis wondrous strange, such spectacles
Are rare i'th' Court, and they were to skirmish naked
Before her, then there might be some excuse.
There is gimcracks in't, the Queen is wise
Above her years.

PHILOCLES
Macarius is perplex'd.

[Enter **EUBULUS**.

LISIMACHUS
I cannot blame him, but my Lord Eubulus
Returns, they are both troubled, 'las good men,
But our duties are expected, we forget.

[Exit **PHILOCLES**

EUBULUS
I must resolve, and yet things are not ripe,
My brains upon the torture.

MACARIUS
This may quit
The hazard of his person, whose least drop
Of blood, is worth more than our families.
My Lord Eubulus, I have thought a way
To stay the young mens desperate proceedings,
It is our cause they fight, let us beseech
The Queen, to grant us two the priviledge
Of Duel, rather than expose their lives
To eithers fury; it were pity they
Should run upon so black a destiny,
We are both old, and may be spar'd, a pair
Of fruitless trees, mossie, and wither'd trunks,
That fill up too much room.

EUBULUS
Most willingly,

And I will praise her charity to allow it;
I have not yet forgot to use a sword,
Let's lose no time, by this act, she will licence
Our souls to leave our bodies but a day,
Perhaps an hour the sooner; they may live
To do her better service, and be friends
When we are dead, and yet I have no hope
This will be granted, curse upon our faction.

MACARIUS
If she deny us—

EUBULUS
What?

MACARIUS
I wou'd do somewhat—

EUBULUS
There's something o' th' suddain struck upon
My imagination that may secure us.

MACARIUS
Name it, if no dishonor wait upon't
To preserve them, I'll accept any danger.

EUBULUS
There is no other way, and yet my heart
Would be excus'd, but 'tis to save his life.

MACARIUS
Speak it Eubulus.

EUBULUS
In your ear I shall,
It sha'not make a noise if you refuse it.

MACARIUS
Hum? though it stir my bloud, I'll meet Arcadius,
If this preserve thee not, I must unseal
Another mistery.

[Exit.

[Enter **QUEEN**, **LISIMACHUS**, **CASSANDER**, **CHARILLA**, **LISANDER**, **PHILOCLES**, **ANTIGONUS**.

QUEEN
We owe to all your loves, and will deserve

At least by our endeavours, that none may
This day repent their prayers, my Lord Protector.

CASSANDER
Madam, I have no
Such Title now, and am blest to lose
That name so happily: I was but trusted
With a glorious burden.

QUEEN
You have prov'd
Your self our faithful Counsellor, and must still
Protect our growing state: a Kingdoms Scepter
Weighs down a womans arm, this Crown sits heavy
Upon my brow already, and we know
There's something more than mettal in this wreath,
Of shining glory, but your faith, and counsel,
That are familiar with mysteries,
And depths of state, have power to make us fit
For such a bearing, in which both you shall
Doe loyal service, and reward your Duties.

CASSANDER
Heaven preserve your Highness.

QUEEN
But yet my Lords and Gentlemen, let none
Mistake me, that because I urge your wisdoms,
I shall grow careless, and impose on you
The managing of this great Province, no,
We will be active too, and as we are
In dignity above your persons, so,
The greatest portion of the difficulties
We call to us, you in your several places
Relieving us with your experience,
Observing in your best directions
All modesty, and distance; for although
We are but young, no action shall forfeit
Our royal priviledge, or encourage any
Too unreverent boldness; as it will become
Our honor to consult, e'r we determine
Of the most necessary things of state,
So we are sensible of a check,
But in a brow, that saucily controuls
Our action, presuming on our years
As few, or frailty of our sex; that head
Is not secure, that dares our power or justice.

PHILOCLES
She has a brave spirit, look how the Protector
Grows pale already.

QUEEN
But I speak to you
Are perfect in obedience, and may spare
This Theme, yet 'twas no immateriall
Part of our character, since I desire
All should take notice, I have studied
The knowledge of my self, by which I shall
Better distinguish of your worth and persons
In your relations to us.

LISIMACHUS
This language
Is but a threatening to some body.

QUEEN
But we miss some, that use not to absent
Their duties from us, where's Macarius?

CASSANDER
Retir'd to grieve, your Majesty hath given
Consent, Arcadius should enter the List
To day with young Seleucus.

QUEEN
We purpose

[Enter **GENTLEMAN**.

They shall proceed, what's he?

PHILOCLES
A Gentleman belonging to Seleucus that gives notice
He is prepar'd, and waits your royal pleasure.

QUEEN
He was compos'd for action, give notice
To Arcadius, and admit the challenger:
Let other Princes boast their gaudy tilting,
And mockery of battles, but our triumph
Is celebrated with true noble valour.

[Enter **SELEUCUS**, **ARCADIUS**, at several doors, their **PAGES** before them, bearing their Targets.

Two young men spirited enough to have

Two kingdoms staked upon their swords, Lisimachus
Do not they excellently become their arms?
'Twere pity but they should do something more
Then wave their plumes.

[A **SHOUT** within.
What noise is that?

[Enter **MACARIUS**, and **EUBULUS**.

MACARIUS
The peoples joy to know us reconcil'd,
Is added to the jubile of the day,
We have no more a faction but one heart,
Peace flow in every bosom.

EUBULUS
Throw away
These instruments of death, and like two friends
Embrace by our example.

QUEEN
This unfein'd?

MACARIUS
By our duties to your self, dear Madam
Command them not advance, our houses from
This minute are incorporated; happy day
Our eyes at which before revenge look'd forth,
May clear suspition, oh my Arcadius!

EUBULUS
We have found a nearer way to friendship, Madam,
Than by exposing them to fight for us.

QUEEN
If this be faithful, our desires are blest.
We had no thought to waste, but reconcile
Your bloud this way, and we did prophesie
This happy chance, spring into eithers bosom,
Arcadius and Seleucus, what can now
Be added to this days felicity?
Yes, there is something, is there not my Lord?
While we are Virgin Queen.

CASSANDER
Ha, that string
Doth promise Musick.

QUEEN
I am yet my Lords
Your single joy, and when I look upon,
What I have took, to manage the great care
Of this most flourishing kingdom, I incline
To think I shall do justice to my self,
If I choose one, whose strength and virtue may
Assist my undertaking, think you Lords,
A Husband would not help?

LISIMACHUS
No question, Madam,
And he that you purpose to make so blest
Must needs be worthy of our humblest duty,
It is the general vote.

QUEEN
We will not then
Trouble Ambassadors to treat with any
Princes abroad, within our own dominion,
Fruitful in honor, we shall make our choice;
And that we may not keep you over long
In the imagination, from this circle, we
Have purpose to elect; one, whom I shall
Salute a King and Husband.

LISANDER
Now my Lord Lisimachus.

QUEEN
Nor shall we in this action be accus'd
Of rashness, since the man we shall declare
Deserving our affection, hath been early
In our opinion, which had reason first
To guide it, and his known nobility
Long marry'd to our thoughts, will justifie
Our fair election.

PHILOCLES
Lisimachus blushes.

CASSANDER
Direct our duties, Madam, to pray for him.

QUEEN
Arcadius, you see from whence we come,
Pray lead us back, you may ascend.

[She comes from the State.

CASSANDER
How's this? o're-reach'd?

ARCADIUS
Madam, be charitable to your humblest creature,
Doe not reward the heart, that falls in duty
Beneath your feet, with making me the burden
Of the Court-mirth, a mockery for Pages,
'Twere Treason in me but to think you meane thus.

QUEEN
Arcadius, you must refuse my love,
Or shame this Kingdom.

PHILOCLES
Is the wind in that corner?

CASSANDER
I shall run mad Lisimachus.

LISIMACHUS
Sir, contain your self.

SELEUCUS
Is this to be believ'd?

MACARIUS
What dream is this?

PHILOCLES
He kisses her, now by this day I am glad on't.

LISANDER
Mark the Protector.

ANTIGONUS
Let him fret his heart-strings.

QUEEN
Is the day cloudy on the sudden?

ARCADIUS
Gentlemen,
It was not my ambition, I durst never
Aspire so high in thought, but since her Majesty

Hath pleas'd to call me to this honor, I
Will study to be worthy of her grace,
By whom I live.

QUEEN
The Church to morrow shall
Confirme our marriage, noble Lisimachus;
We'll find out other wayes to recompence
Your love to us, set forward, come Arcadius.

MACARIUS
It must be so, and yet let me consider.

CASSANDER
He insults already, policy assist me,
To break his neck.

LISIMACHUS
Who would trust Woman?
Lost in a pair of minutes, lost, how bright
A morning rose, but now, and now 'tis night?

[Exeunt.

ACTUS TERTIUS

SCÆNA PRIMA

Enter **POLIDORA**, and a **SERVANT**.

POLIDORA
Oh where shall Virgins look for faith hereafter?
If he prove false, after so many vowes?
And yet if I consider, he was tempted
Above the strength of a young Lover, two
Such glorious courting his acceptance, were
Able to make disloyalty no sin,
At least not seem a fault, a Lady first,
Whose very looks would thaw a man more frozen
Than the Alps, quicken a soul more dead than Winter,
Add to her beauty and perfection,
That she's a Queen, and brings with her a Kingdom
Able to make a great mind forfeit Heaven.
What could the frailty of Arcadius
Suggest, to unspirit him so much, as not
To fly to her embraces, you were present

When she declar'd her self.

SERVANT
Yes Madam.

POLIDORA
Tell me,
Did not he make a pause, when the fair Queen
A full temptation stood him?

SERVANT
Very little
My judgment could distinguish, she did no sooner
Propound, but he accepted.

POLIDORA
That was ill,
He might with honor stand one or two minutes,
Me thinks it should have startled him a little,
To have rememberd me, I have deserv'd
At least a cold thought, well, pray give it him.

SERVANT
I shall.

POLIDORA
When?

SERVANT
Instantly.

POLIDORA
Not so,
But take a time when his joy swels him most,
When his delights are high and ravishing,
When you perceive his Soul dance in his eyes,
When she that must be his hath drest her beauty,
With all her pride, and sends a thousand Cupids
To call him to the tasting of her lip;
Then give him this, and tell him, while I live,
I'll pray for him.

SERVANT
I shall.

[Exeunt.

[Enter **CASSANDER**, and **LISIMACHUS**.

CASSANDER
There is no way but death.

LISIMACHUS
That's black, and horrid,
Consider, Sir, it was her sin, not his;
I cannot accuse him, what man could carry
A heart so frozen, not to melt at such
A glorious flame? Who could not fly to such
A happiness?

CASSANDER
Have you ambition
To be a tame fool? see so vast an injury
And not revenge it? make me not suspect
Thy Mother for this sufferance, my Son.

LISIMACHUS
Pray hear me, Sir.

CASSANDER
Hear a patient gull,
A property, thou hast no blood of mine,
If this affront provoke thee not, how canst
Be charitable to thy self, and let him live
To glory in thy shame? Nor is he innocent;
He had before crept slily into her bosome,
And practised thy dishonor.

LISIMACHUS
You begin to stir me, Sir.

CASSANDER
How else could she be guilty
Of such contempt of thee? and in the eye
Of all the Kingdom, they conspir'd this stain,
When they had cunning meetings, shall thy love
And blooming hopes be scatter'd thus, and Lisimachus
Stand idle gazer?

LISIMACHUS
What, Sir, will his death
Advantage us, if she be false to me?
So irreligious, and to touch her person—
Pause, we may be observed.

[Enter **PHILOCLES**, and **LISANDER**.

LISANDER
'Tis the Protector
And his son.

PHILOCLES
Alas, poor Gentleman, I pitty
His neglect, but am not sorry for his Father.
'Tis a strange turne.

LISANDER
The whirligigs of Women.

PHILOCLES
Your Graces servant.

CASSANDER
I am yours Gentlemen,
And should be happy to deserve your loves.

PHILOCLES
Now he can flatter.

LISANDER
In't Sir, to inlarge your sufferings, I have
A heart doth wish
The Queen had known better to reward
Your love and merit.

LISANDER
If you would express
Your love to me, pray do not mention it,
I must obey my fate.

PHILOCLES
She will be married
To t'other Gentleman for certain then?

CASSANDER
I hope you'll wish 'em joy.

PHILOCLES
Indeed I will, Sir.

LISANDER
Your Graces servant

[Exit.

CASSANDER
We are grown
Ridiculous, the pastime of the Court:
Here comes another.

[Enter **SELEUCUS**.

SELEUCUS
Where's your Son, my Lord?

CASSANDER
Like a neglected servant of his Mistress.

SELEUCUS
I would ask him a question.

CASSANDER
What?

SELEUCUS
Whether the Queen,
As 'tis reported, lov'd him, he can tell
Whether she promis'd what they talke of, marriage.

CASSANDER
I can resolve you that, Sir.

SELEUCUS
She did promise?

CASSANDER
Yes.

SELEUCUS
Then shee's a Woman, and your Son;

CASSANDER
What?

SELEUCUS
Not worthy his blood, and expectation,
If he be calme.

CASSANDER
There's no opposing destiny.

SELEUCUS

I would cut the Throat.

CASSANDER
Whose throat?

SELEUCUS
The destinies, that's all, your pardon, Sir,
I am Seleucus still, a poor shadow
Oth' World, a walking picture, it concerns
Not me, I am forgotten by my stars.

CASSANDER
The Queen, with more discretion, might ha chosen Thee.

SELEUCUS
Whom?

CASSANDER
Thee, Seleucus.

SELEUCUS
Me? I cannot dance, and frisk with due activity,
My body is lead, I have too much phlegme, what should
I do with a Kingdome? no, Arcadius
Becomes the cushion, and can please, yet setting
Aside the trick that Ladies of Blood look at,
Another Man might make a shift to weare
Rich Clothes, sit in the chair of state, and nod,
Dare venture on discourse, that does not trench
On compliment, and think the study of Armes
And Arts, more commendable in a Gentleman,
Than any Galliard.

CASSANDER
Arcadius,
And you, were reconcil'd.

SELEUCUS
We? yes, oh yes,
But 'tis not manners now to say we are friends,
At our equality there had been reason,
But now subjection is the word.

CASSANDER
They are not
Yet married.

SELEUCUS

I'll make no Oath upon't,
My Lord Lisimachus,
A word, you'll not be angry if I love you,
May not a Batchellor be made a Cuckold?

LISIMACHUS
How, Sir?

CASSANDER
Lisimachus, this Gentleman
Is worth our embrace, hee's spirited,
And may be useful.

SELEUCUS
Hark you, can you tell
Where's the best Dancing-master? and you mean
To rise at Court, practise to caper, farewel
The noble science, that makes work for cutlers,
It will be out of fashion to weare swords,
Masques, and devices welcome, I salute you,
Is it not pitty any division
Should be heard out of Musick? Oh 'twill be
An excellent age of crotchets; and of Canters.
Buy Captains, that like fools will spend your blood
Out of your Country, you will be of less
Use than your feathers, if you return unman'd
You shall be beaten soon to a new march,
When you shall think it a discretion
To sell your glorious buffes to buy fine pumps,
And pantables, this is I hope no treason.

[Enter **ARCADIUS** leading the **QUEEN**, **CHARILLA**, **EUBULUS**, **LISANDER**, **PHILOCLES**, **POLIDORA**, **SERVANT**.

CASSANDER
Wot stay Lisimachus?

LISIMACHUS
Yes, Sir,
And shew a patience above her injury.

ARCADIUS
This honor is too much, Madam, assume
Your place, and let Arcadius waite still:
'Tis happiness enough to be your servant.

CASSANDER
Now he dissembles.

QUEEN
Sir, you must sit.

ARCADIUS
I am obedient.

QUEEN
This is not Musick
Sprightly enough, it feeds the soul with melancholy.
How sayes Arcadius?

ARCADIUS
Give me leave to think
There is no harmony but in your voice,
And not an accent of your heavenly tongue,
But strikes me into rapture, I incline
To think, the tale of Orpheus no fable,
'Tis possible he might inchant the Rocks,
And charme the Forrest, soften hell, hell it self,
With his commanding Lute, it is no miracle
To what you work, whose very breath conveyes
The hearer into Heaven, how at your lips,
Day-winds gather Perfumes, proudly glide away,
To disperse sweetness round about the world.

SELEUCUS
Fine stuff.

QUEEN
You cannot flatter.

ARCADIUS
Not, if I should say,
Nature had plac'd you here the creatures wonder,
And her own spring, from which all excellence
On Earth's deriv'd, and copyed forth, and when
The character of fair, and good in others
Is quite worne out, and lost, looking on you
It is supply'd, and you alone made mortal
To feed, and keep alive all beauty.

SELEUCUS
Ha, ha, Can you indure it Gentlemen?

LISANDER
What do you meane?

SELEUCUS
Nay, ask him what he meanes, mine is a down
Right laugh.

QUEEN
Well, Sir, proceed.

ARCADIUS
At such bright eyes the stars do light themselves,
At such a forehead Swans renew their white,
From such a lip the morning gathers blushes.

SELEUCUS
The morning is more modest than thy praises,
What a thing does he make her?

ARCADIUS
And when you flie to Heaven and leave this world
No longer maintenance of goodness from you:
Then Poetry shall lose all use with us,
And be no more, since nothing in your absence
Is left, that can be worthy of a Verse.

SELEUCUS
Ha, ha.

QUEEN
Whose that?

SELEUCUS
'Twas I, Madam.

ARCADIUS
Seleucus?

CASSANDER
Ha?

SELEUCUS
Yes, Sir, 'twas I that laugh'd.

ARCADIUS
At what?

SELEUCUS
At nothing.

LISANDER

Contain your self, Seleucus.

EUBULUS
Are you mad?

QUEEN
Have you ambition to be punish'd, Sir?

SELEUCUS
I need not, 'twas punishment
Enough to hear him make an Idol of you, he left
Out the commendation of your patience, I was a little
Mov'd in my nature, to hear his Rodomontados, and
Make a monster of his Mistress, which I pitty'd first,
But seeing him proceed, I guest he brought you
Mirth with his inventions, and so made bold to laugh at it.

QUEEN
You are sawcy,
We'll place you where you sha'not be so merry,
Take him away.

LISANDER
Submit your self.

ARCADIUS
Let me plead for his pardon.

SELEUCUS
I wo'd not owe my life so poorly, beg thy own,
When you are King you cannot bribe your destiny.

EUBULUS
Good Madam hear me, I fear he is distracted,
Brave boy, thou should'st be Master of a soul
Like his: thy honors more concern'd.

SELEUCUS
'Tis charity,
A way wo' mee, 'boy Madam?

CASSANDER
He has a daring spirit.

[Exit **SELEUCUS**, **EUBULUS**.

ARCADIUS
These, and a thousand more affronts I must

Expect: your favors draw them all upon me;
In my first state I had no enemies,
I was secure, while I did grow beneath
This expectation, humble valleys thrive with
Their bosomes full of flowers, when the Hills melt
With lightning, and rough anger of the clouds,
Let me retire.

QUEEN
And can Arcadius
At such a breath be mov'd, I had opinion
Your courage durst have stood a tempest for
Our love, can you for this incline to leave
What other Princes should in vain have sued for?
How many Lovers are in Epire now
Would throw themselves on danger, not expect
One enemy, but empty their own veins,
And think the loss of all their blood rewarded,
To have one smile of us when they are dying?
And shall this murmur shake you?

ARCADIUS
Not dear Madam,
My life is such a poor despised thing,
In value your least graces, that
To lose it were to make my self a victory,
It is not for my self, I fear: the envy
Of others cannot fasten wound in me
Greater, than that your goodness should be check'd
So daringly.

QUEEN
Let not those thoughts afflict thee,
While we have power to correct the offences,
Arcadius be mine, this shall confirm it.

ARCADIUS
I shall forget,
And lose my way to heaven, that touch had been
Enough to have restor'd me, and infus'd
A spirit of a more celestial nature,
After the tedious absence of my soul,
Oh bless me not too much, one smile a day
Would stretch my life to mortality;
Poets that wrap divinity in tales,
Look here, and give your coppies forth of angels,
What blessing can remain?

QUEEN
Our Marriage.

ARCADIUS
Place then some horrors in the way
For me, not you, to pass, the journeys end
Holds out such glories to me, I should think
Hell but a poor degree of suffering for it,
What's that, some petition? a Letter to me.
You had a Polidora, ha, that's all.
Ith' minute when my vessels new lanch'd forth,
With all my pride, and silken wings about me
I strike upon a Rock: What power can save me?
You had a Polidora; there's a name
Kill'd with grief, I can so soon forget her.

SERVANT
She did impose on me this service, Sir,
And while she lives she sayes, shee'll pray for you.

ARCADIUS
She lives,
That's well, and yet 'twere better, for my fame,
And honor, she were dead; What fate hath plac'd me
Upon this fearful precipice?

SERVANT
He's troubled.

ARCADIUS
I must resolve, my faith is violated
Already, yet poor loving Polidora
Will pray for me, she sayes, to think she can
Render me hated to my self, and every
Thought's a tormentor, let me then be just.

QUEEN
Arcadius.

ARCADIUS
That voice prevailes agen, oh Polidora,
Thou must forgive Arcadius, I dare not
Turn rebel to a Princess, I shall love
Thy vertue, but a Kingdom has a charme
To excuse our frailty, dearest Madam.

QUEEN
Now set forward.

ARCADIUS
To perfect all our joyes.

[Enter **MACARIUS**, and a **BISHOP**, **CASSANDER**.

MACARIUS
I'll fright their glories.

CASSANDER
By what means?

MACARIUS
Observe.

ARCADIUS
Our good Unckle, welcome.

QUEEN
My Lord Macarius, we did want your person,
There's something in our joyes wherein you share.

MACARIUS
This you intend your highness wedding day.

QUEEN
We are going.

MACARIUS
Save you labor
I have brought a Priest to meet you.

ARCADIUS
Reverend Father.

QUEEN
Meet us, Why?

MACARIUS
To tell you, that you must not Marry.

CASSANDER
Didst thou hear that, Lisimachus?

LISIMACHUS
And wonder what will follow.

QUEEN

We must not marry.

BISHOP
Madam, 'tis a rule
First made in heaven, and I must needs declare
You and Arcadius must tie no knot
Of Man and Wife.

ARCADIUS
Is my Unckle mad?

QUEEN
Joy has transported him,
Or age has made him dote, Macarius
Provoke us not too much, you will presume
Above our mercy.

MACARIUS
I'll discharge my duty,
Could your frown strike me dead, my Lord, you know
Whose character this is.

CASSANDER
It is Theodosius,
Your graces Father.

BISHOP
I am subscribed a witness.

PHILOCLES
Upon my life 'tis his.

MACARIUS
Fear not, I'll cross this Match.

CASSANDER
I'll bless thee for't.

ARCADIUS
Unckle, d'ee know what you do, or what we are
Going to finish? you will not break the neck of my glorious
Fortune, now my foots ith' stirrup, and mounting,
Throw me over the saddle? I hope you'll let one
Be a King, Madam, 'tis as you say,
My Unckle is something craz'd, there's a worm
In's brain, but I beseech you pardon him, he is
Not the first of your counsel, that has talk'd
Idly, d'ee hear my Lord Bishop, I hope

You have more Religion than to joyn with him
To undoe me.

BISHOP
Not I Sir, but I am commanded by oath,
And conscience to speak truth.

ARCADIUS
If your truth should do me any harm, I shall never
Be in charity with a Croziers staffe, look too't.

QUEEN
My youngest Brother.

CASSANDER
Worse and worse, my brains.

[Exit.

MACARIUS
Deliver'd to me an Infant with this writing,
To which this reverend Father is a witness.

LISANDER
This he whom we so long thought dead, a childe?

QUEEN
But what should make my Father to trust him
To your concealment? give abroad his death, and bury
An empty coffin?

MACARIUS
A jealousie he had
Upon Cassander, whose ambitious brain
He fear'd would make no conscience to depose
His son, to make Lisimachus King of Epire.

QUEEN
He made no scruple to expose me then
To any danger?

MACARIUS
He secur'd you, Madam,
By an early Engagement of your affection
To Lisimachus, exempt this testimony,
Had he been Arcadius, and my Nephew,
I needed not obtrude him on the state,
Your love and marriage had made him King

Without my trouble, and sav'd that ambition,
There was necessity to open now
His birth, and title.

PHILOCLES
Demetrius alive.

ARCADIUS
What riddles are these, Whom do they talk of?

OMNES
Congratulate your return to life, and honor,
And as becomes us, with one voice salute you,
Demetrius King of Epire.

MACARIUS
I am no Uncle, Sir, this is your Sister,
I should have suffer'd incest to have kept you
Longer ith' dark: love, and be happy both,
My trust is now discharg'd.

LISANDER
And we rejoyce.

ARCADIUS
But do not mock me, Gentlemen,
May I be bold upon your words to say
I am Prince Theodosius Son?

MACARIUS
The King.

ARCADIUS
You'll justifie it?
Sister, I am very glad to see you.

SOPHIA
I am to find a brother, and resign my glory,
My triumph is my shame.

[Exit.

[Enter **CASSANDER**.

CASSANDER
Thine ear Lisimachus.

ARCADIUS

Gentlemen I owe
Unto your loves, as large acknowledgment
As to my birth, for this great honor, and
My study shall be equal to be thought
Worthy of both.

CASSANDER
Thou art turn'd Marble.

LISIMACHUS
There will be the less charge for my Monument.

CASSANDER
This must not be, sit fast young King.

[Exit.

LISIMACHUS
Your sister, Sir, is gone.

ARCADIUS
My sister should have been my Bride, that name
Puts me in mind of Polidora, ha?
Lisander, Philocles, Gentlemen,
If you will have me think your hearts allow me
Theodosius son, oh quickly snatch some wings,
Express it in your haste to Polidora,
Tell her what title is new dropt from heaven
To make her rich; onely created for me:
Give her the ceremony of my Queen,
With all the state that may become our Bride,
Attend her to this throne; Are you not there?
Yet stay, 'tis too much pride to send for her,
Wee'll go our self, no honor is enough
For Polidora, to redeem our fault,
Salute her gently from me, and, upon
Your knee, present her with this Diadem,
'Tis our first gift, tell her Demetrius follows
To be her guest, and give himself a servant
To her chast bosome, bid her stretch her heart
To meet me, I am lost in joy and wonder.

[Exeunt **OMNES**.

ACTUS QUARTUS

SCÆNA PRIMA

Enter **CASSANDER, EUBULUS, SOLDIER.**

CASSANDER
Where's the Captain of the Castle?

SOLDIER
Hee'll attend your honors presently.

CASSANDER
Give him knowledge we expect him.

SOLDIER
I shall, my Lord.

[Exit.

CASSANDER
He is my creature, fear not,
And shall run any course that we propound.

EUBULUS
My Lord, I like the substance of your plot,
'Tis promising, but matters of this consequence
Are not so easily perfect, and it does
Concern our heads to build upon secure
Principles, though Seleucus, I confess,
Carry a high, and daring spirit in him,
'Tis hard to thrust upon the state new setled
Any impostor, and we know not yet
Whether hee'll undertake to play the Prince;
Or if he should accept it, with what cunning
He can behave himself.

CASSANDER
My Lord, affairs
Of such a glorious nature, are half finish'd,
When they begin with confidence.

EUBULUS
Admit
He want no art, nor courage, it must rest
Upon the people to receive his title,
And with what danger their uncertain breath
May flatter ours, Demetrius scarcely warm
In the Kings seat, I may suspect.

CASSANDER
That reason
Makes for our part, for if it be so probable,
That young Demetrius should be living, Why
May not we work them to believe, Leonatus,
The eldest son was, by some trick, preserv'd,
And now would claim his own: there were two sons,
Who in their Fathers life we supposed dead,
May not we find a circumstance to make
This seem as clear as t'other, let the vulgar
Be once possest, wee'll carry Epire from
Demetrius, and the World.

EUBULUS
I could be pleas'd
To see my Son a King.

[Enter **POLEANUS**.

The Captain's here.

POLEANUS
I waite your Lordships pleasure.

CASSANDER
We come to visit your late prisoner:
I will not doubt, but you intreat him fairly,
He will deserve it for himself, and you
Be fortunate in any occasion,
To have exprest your service.

POLEANUS
Sir, the knowledge
Of my honorable Lord his Father, will
Instruct me to behave my self with all
Respects becoming me, to such a son.

CASSANDER
These things will least
Oblige you, but how bears he his restraint?

POLEANUS
As one whose soul's above it.

EUBULUS
Patiently?

POLEANUS

With contempt rather of the great command
Which made him prisoner, he will talke sometimes
So strangely to himself.

EUBULUS
Hee's here.

[Enter **SELEUCUS**.

SELEUCUS
Why was I born to be a subject? 'tis
Soon answer'd, sure my Father was no Prince,
That's all: the same ingredients use to make
A Man, as active, though not royal blood
Went to my composition, and I
Was gotten with as good a will perhaps,
And my birth cost my Mother as much sorrow,
As I had been born an Emperor.

CASSANDER
While I look
Upon him, something in his face presents
A King indeed.

EUBULUS
He does resemble much
Theodosius too.

CASSANDER
Whose son we would pretend him,
This will advance our plot.

SELEUCUS
'Tis but a name,
And mere opinion, that prefers one man
Above another, I'll imagine then
I am a Prince, or some brave thing on Earth,
And see what follows: but it must not be,
My single voice will carry it, the name
Of King must be attended with a troop
Of acclamations, on whose ayrie wings
He mounts, and once exalted, threatens Heaven,
And all the stars: how to acquire this noise,
And be the thing I talke of, men have risen
From a more cheap nobility to Empires,
From dark originals, and sordid blood,
Nay some that had no fathers, sons of the earth,
And flying people, have aspir'd to Kingdoms,

Made nations tremble, and have practis'd frowns
To awe the world, their memory is glorious,
And I would hug them in their shades, but what's
All this to me, that am I know not what,
And less in expectation?

POLEANUS
Are you serious?

CASSANDER
Will you assist, and run a fate with us.

POLEANUS
Command my life, I owe it to your favor.

SELEUCUS
Arcadius was once as far from being
As I, and had we not so cunningly
Been reconcil'd, or one, or both had gone
To seek our fortunes in another world;
What's the device now? If my death be next,
The summons shall not make me once look pale.

CASSANDER
Chide your too vain suspitions, we bring
A life, and liberty, with what else can make
Thy ambition happy, th'ast a glorious flame,
We come to advance it.

SELEUCUS
How?

CASSANDER
Have but a will,
And be what thy own thoughts dare prompt thee to,
A King.

SELEUCUS
You do not mock me Gentlemen?
You are my Father, Sir.

EUBULUS
This minute shall
Declare it, my Seleucus, our hearts swell'd
With joy, with duty rather, oh my boy!

SELEUCUS
What's the mistery?

POLEANUS
You must be a King.

CASSANDER
Seleucus, stay, thou art too incredulous,
Let not our faith, and study to exalt thee,
Be so rewarded.

EUBULUS
I pronounce thee King,
Unless thy spirit be turn'd coward, and
Thou faint to accept it.

SELEUCUS
King of what?

CASSANDER
Of Epire.

SELEUCUS
Although the Queen, since she sent me hither,
Were gone to Heaven I know not how,
That title could devolve to me.

CASSANDER
We have
No Queen, since he that should have married her,
Is prov'd her youngest brother, and now King
In his own title.

SELEUCUS
Thank you Gentlemen,
There's hope for me.

CASSANDER
Why, you dare fight with him
And need be, for the Kingdom.

SELEUCUS
With Arcadius?
If you'll make stakes, my life against his crown,
I'll fight with him, and you, and your fine Son,
And all the Courtiers one after another.

CASSANDER
'Two'not come to that.

SELEUCUS
I am of your Lordships mind, so fare you well.

CASSANDER
Yet stay and hear—

SELEUCUS
What? that you have betray'd me:
Do, tell your King, my life is grown a burden,
And I'll confess, and make your souls look pale,
To see how nimble mine shall leap this battlement
Of flesh, and dying, laugh at your poor malice.

OMNES
No more, long live Leonatus King of Epire.

SELEUCUS
Leonatus, Who's that?

CASSANDER
Be bold, and be a King, our brains have been
Working to raise you to this height, here are
None but friends, dare you but call your self
Leonatus, and but justifie with confidence
What we'll proclaime you, if we do not bring
The Crown to your head, we will forfeit ours.

EUBULUS
The state is in distraction, Arcadius
Is prov'd a King, there was an elder brother,
If you dare but pronounce, you are the same,
Forget you are my son.

POLEANUS
These are no trifles, Sir, all is plotted,
To assure your greatness; if you will be wise,
And take the faire occasion that's presented.

SELEUCUS
Arcadius, you say, is lawful King,
And now to depose him, you would make me
An elder brother, is't not so?

CASSANDER
Most right.

SELEUCUS
Nay, right or wrong, if this be your true meaning.

OMNES
Upon our lives.

SELEUCUS
I'll venture mine, but with your pardon,
Whose brain was this? from whom took this plot life?

EUBULUS
My Lord Cassander.

SELEUCUS
And you are of his mind? and you? and think
This may be done?

EUBULUS
The destinies shall not cross us, if you have
Spirit to undertake it.

SELEUCUS
Undertake it?
I am not us'd to compliment, I'll owe
My life to you, my fortunes to your Lordship,
Compose me as you please, and when y'ave made
Me what you promise, you shall both divide
Me equally: one word, my Lord, I had rather
Live in the prison still, than be a propency
To advance his politick ends.

EUBULUS
Have no suspition.

CASSANDER
So, so, I see Demetrius heels already
Trip'd up, and I'll dispatch him out oth' way,
Which gone, I can depose this at my leasure,
Being an Impostor, then my Son stands fair,
And may piece with the Princess, we lose time,
What think you, if we first surprize the Court?
While you command the Castle, we shall curbe
All opposition.

EUBULUS
Let's proclaim him first,
I have some faction, the people love me,
They gain'd to us, wee'll fall upon the Court.

CASSANDER

Unless Demetrius yield himself, he bleeds.

SELEUCUS
Who dares call treason sin, when it succeeds?

[Exeunt **OMNES**.

[Enter **SOPHIA**, and **CHARILLA**.

CHARILLA
Madam, you are too passionate, and lose
The greatness of your soul, with the expence
Of too much grief, for that which providence
Hath eas'd you of, the burden of a state
Above your tender bearing.

SOPHIA
Thour't a fool,
And canst not reach the spirit of a Lady,
Born great as I was, and made onely less
By a too cruel destiny, above
Our tender bearing: What goes richer to
The composition of Man, than ours?
Our soul as free, and spatious; our heart's
As great, our will as large, each thought as active,
And in this onely Man more proud than we,
That would have us less capable of Empire,
But search the stories, and the name of Queen
Shines bright with glory, and some precedents
Above Mans imitation.

CHARILLA
I grant it
For the honor of our sex, nor have you, Madam,
By any weakness, forfeited command,
He that succeeds, in justice, was before you,
And you have gain'd more, in a royal brother,
Than you could lose by your resign of Epire.

SOPHIA
This I allow Charilla, I ha done;
'Tis not the thought I am depos'd afflicts me,
At the same time I feel a joy to know
My Brother living: no, there is another
Wound in me above cure.

CHARILLA
Virtue forbid.

SOPHIA
Canst find me out a Surgeon for that?

CHARILLA
For what?

SOPHIA
My bleeding fame.

CHARILLA
Oh do not injure
Your own clear innocence.

SOPHIA
Do not flatter me,
I have been guilty of an act, will make
All love in women question'd, is not that
A blot upon a Virgins name? my birth
Cannot extenuate my shame, I am
Become the stain of Epire.

CHARILLA
'Tis but
Your own opinion, Madam, which presents
Something to fright your self, which cannot
Be in the same shape so horrid to our sense.

SOPHIA
Thou wod'st, but canst not appear ignorant:
Did not the Court, nay, the whole Kingdom, take
Notice, I lov'd Lisimachus?

CHARILLA
True, Madam.

SOPHIA
No, I was false,
Though counsel'd by my Father to affect him,
I had my politick ends upon Cassander,
To be absolute Queen, flattering his son with hopes
Of love and marriage, when that very day
I blush to think I wrong'd Lisimachus,
That noble Gentleman, but heaven punish'd me;
For though to know Demetrius was a blessing,
Yet who will not impute it my dishonor.

CHARILLA

Madam, you yet may recompence Lisimachus,
If you affect him now, you were not false
To him, whom then you lov'd not, if you can
Find any gentle passion in your soul
To entertain his thought, no doubt his heart,
Though sad retains a noble will to meet it,
His love was firm to you, and cannot be
Unrooted with one storme.

SOPHIA
He will not sure
Trust any language from her tongue that mock'd him,
Although my soul doth weep for't, and is punish'd
To love him above the world.

[Enter **LISIMACHUS**.

CHARILLA
Hee's here
As fate would have him reconcil'd, be free,
And speak your thoughts.

LISIMACHUS
If, Madam, I appear
Too bold, your charity will sign my pardon:
I heard you were not well, which made me haste
To pay the duty of an humble visit.

SOPHIA
You do not mock me, Sir.

LISIMACHUS
I am confident
You think me not so lost to manners, in
The knowledge of your person, to bring with me
Such rudeness, I have nothing to present,
But a heart full of wishes for your health,
And what else may be added to your happiness.

SOPHIA
I thought you had been sensible.

LISIMACHUS
How Madam?

SOPHIA
A man of understanding, can you spend
One prayer for me, remembring the dishonor

I have done Lisimachus?

LISIMACHUS
Nothing can deface that part of my
Religion in me, not to pray for you.

SOPHIA
It is not then impossible you may
Forgive me too, indeed I have a soul
Is full of penitence, and something else,
If blushing would allow to give't a name.

LISIMACHUS
What Madam?

SOPHIA
Love, a love that should redeem
My past offence, and make me white again.

LISIMACHUS
I hope no sadness can possess your thoughts
For me, I am not worthy of this sorrow,
But if you mean it any satisfaction
For what your will hath made me suffer, 'tis
But a strange overflow of Charity,
To keep me still alive, be your self Madam,
And let no cause of mine, be guilty of
This rape upon your eyes, my name's not worth
The least of all your tears.

SOPHIA
You think 'em counterfeit.

LISIMACHUS
Although I may
Suspect a Womans smile hereafter, yet
I would believe their wet eyes, and if this
Be what you promise, for my sake, I have
But one reply.

SOPHIA
I waite it.

LISIMACHUS
I have now
Another Mistress.

SOPHIA

Stay.

LISIMACHUS
To whom I have made
Since your revolt from me, a new chaste vow,
Which not the second malice of my fate
Shall violate, and she deserves it, Madam,
Even for that wherein you are excellent,
Beauty, in which she shines equal to you
Her vertue, if she but maintain what now
She is Mistress of, beyond all competition,
So rich it cannot know to be improv'd,
At least in my esteem, I may offend,
But truth shall justifie, I have not flatter'd her,
I beg your pardon, and to leave, my duty
Upon your hand, all that is good flow in you.

[Exit.

SOPHIA
Did he not say, Charilla, that he had
Another Mistress?

CHARILLA
Such a sound, methought,
Came from him.

SOPHIA
Let's remove, here's too much ayre,
The sad note multiplies.

CHARILLA
Take courage, Madam,
And my advice, he has another Mistress,
If he have twenty, be you wise, and cross him
With entertaining twice as many servants,
And when he sees your humor he'll return.
And sue for any Livery, grieve for this.

SOPHIA
It must be she, 'tis Polidora has
Taken his heart, she live my rival,
How does the thought inflame me!

CHARILLA
Polidora?

SOPHIA

And yet she does but justly, and he too;
I would have rob'd her of Arcadius heart,
And they will both have this revenge on me,
But something will rebel.

[Exit.

[Enter **DEMETRIUS, PHILOCLES, LISANDER**.

DEMETRIUS
The house is desolate, none comes forth to meet us,
Shee's slow to entertain us: Philocles,
I prethee tell me, did she weare no cloud
Upon her brow, was't freely that she said
We should be welcome.

PHILOCLES
To my apprehension,
Yet 'tis my wonder she appears not.

LISANDER
She, nor any other,
Sure there's some conceit
To excuse it.

DEMETRIUS
Stay, Who's this? observe what follows?

PHILOCLES
Fortune? some maske to entertain you, Sir.

[Enter **FORTUNE** crown'd, attended with **YOUTH, HEALTH**, and **PLEASURE**.

FORTUNE
Not yet? What silence doth inhabit here?
No preparation to bid Fortune welcome!
Fortune, the genious of the World, have we
Descended from our pride, and state to come,
So far attended with our darlings, Youth,
Pleasure, and Health, to be neglected thus?
Sure this is not the place? call hither Fame.

[Enter **FAME**.

FAME
What would great Fortune?

FORTUNE

Know,
Who dwells here.

FAME
Once more I report great Queen,
This is the house of Love.

FORTUNE
It cannot be,
This place has too much shade, and looks as if
It had been quite forgotten of the Spring,
And Sun-beames Love, affect society,
And heat, here all is cold as the hairs of Winter,
No harmony, to catch the busie eare
Of passengers, no object of delight,
To take the wandring eyes, no song, no grone
Of Lovers, no complaint of Willow garlands,
Love has a Beacon upon his palace top,
Of flaming hearts, to call the weary pilgrime
To rest, and dwell with him, I see no fire
To threaten, or to warme: Can Love dwell here?

FAME
If there be noble love upon the World,
Trust Fame, and find it here.

FORTUNE
Make good your boast,
And bring him to us.

DEMETRIUS
What does mean all this?

LISANDER
I told you, Sir, we should have some device.

[Enter **LOVE**.

There's Cupid now, that little Gentleman,
Has troubled every Masque at Court this seven year.

DEMETRIUS
No more.

LOVE
Welcome to Love, how much you honor me!
It had become me, that, upon your summons,
I should have waited upon mighty Fortune,

But since you have vouchsafed to visit me;
All the delights Love can invent, shall flow
To entertain you, Musick through the ayre
Shoot your inticing harmony.

FORTUNE
We came to dance and revel with you.

LOVE
I am poor
In my ambition, and want thought to reach
How much you honor Love.

[Dance.

[Enter **HONOR**.

HONOR
What intrusion's this?
Whom do you seek here.

LOVE
'Tis honor.

FORTUNE
He my servant.

LOVE
Fortune is come to visit us.

HONOR
And has
Corrupted Love: Is this thy faith to her,
On whom we both waite, to betray her thus
To Fortunes triumph? take her giddy wheel,
And be no more companion to honor;
I blush to know thee, Who'll believe there can
Be truth in Love hereafter?

LOVE
I have found
My eyes, and see my shame, and with it, this
Proud sorceress, from whom, and all her charmes,
I flye agen to Honor, be my guard,
Without thee I am lost, and cannot boast,
The merit of a name.

FORTUNE

Despis'd? I shall
Remember this affront.

DEMETRIUS
What Moral's this?

[Exeunt.

[Enter **HONOR** with the Crown upon a mourning Cushion.

What melancholly object strikes a sudden
Chillness through all my veines; and turns me Ice?
It is the same I sent, the very same,
As the first pledge of her insuing greatness:
Why in this mourning livery, if she live
To whom I sent it? ha, What shape of sorrow?

[Enter **POLIDORA** in mourning.

It is not Polidora, she was faire
Enough, and wanted not the setting off
With such a black: if thou beest Polidora,
Why mournes my love? it neither does become
Thy fortune, nor my joyes.

POLIDORA
But it becomes
My griefs, this habit fits a funeral,
And it were sin, my Lord, not to lament
A friend new dead.

DEMETRIUS
And I yet living? can
A sorrow enter but upon thy Garment,
Or discomplexion thy attire, whilst I
Enjoy a life for thee? Who can deserve,
Weigh'd with thy living comforts, but a piece
Of all this Ceremony? give him a name.

POLIDORA
He was Arcadius.

DEMETRIUS
Arcadius?

POLIDORA
A Gentleman that lov'd me dearly once,
And does compel these poor, and fruitless drops,

Which willingly would fall upon his hearse,
To imbalme him twice.

DEMETRIUS
And are you sure hee's dead?

POLIDORA
As sure as you'r living, Sir, and yet
I did not close his eyes, but he is dead,
And I shall never see the same Arcadius:
He was a Man so rich in all that's good,
At least I thought him so, so perfect in
The rules of honor, whom alone to imitate
Were glory in a Prince, Nature her self,
Till his creation, wrought imperfectly,
As she had made but tryal of the rest,
To mould him excellent.

DEMETRIUS
And is he dead?
Come, shame him not with praises, recollect
Thy scatter'd hopes, and let me tell my best,
And dearest Polidora, that he lives,
Still lives to honor thee.

POLIDORA
Lives, Where?

DEMETRIUS
Look here.
Am not I worth your knowledge?

POLIDORA
And my duty,
You are Demetrius, King of Epire, Sir.
I could not easily mistake him so,
To whom I gave my heart.

DEMETRIUS
Mine is not chang'd,
But still hath fed upon thy memory,
These honors, and additions of state
Are lent me for thy sake, be not so strange,
Let me not lose my entertainment, now
I am improv'd, and rais'd unto the height,
Beneath which, I did blush to ask thy love.

POLIDORA

Give me your pardon, Sir, Arcadius,
At our last meeting, without argument,
To move him more than his affection to me,
Vow'd he did love me; love me above all Women,
And to confirm his heart, was truely mine,
He wish'd, I tremble to remember it,
When he forsook his Polidora's love,
That Heaven might kill his happiness on Earth:
Was not this nobly said? did not this promise
A truth to shame the Turtles?

DEMETRIUS
And his heart
Is still the same, and I thy constant Lover.

POLIDORA
Give me your leave, I pray, I would not say,
Arcadius was perjur'd, but the same day
Forgetting all his promises, and oathes,
While yet they hung upon his lips, forsook me,
D'ee not remember this too, gave his faith
From me, transported with the noise of greatness,
And would be married to a Kingdom.

DEMETRIUS
But Heaven permitted not I should dispose
What was ordain'd for thee.

POLIDORA
It was not virtue
In him, for sure he found no check, no sting
In his own bosome, but gave freely all
The reines to blind ambition.

DEMETRIUS
I am wounded,
The thought of thee ith' throng of all my joyes,
Like poyson powr'd in Nectar, turnes me frantick:
Dear, if Arcadius have made a fault,
Let not Demetrius be punish'd for't,
He pleads that ever will be constant to thee.

POLIDORA
Shall I believe Mans flatteries agen,
Lose my sweet rest, and peace of thought agen,
Be drawn by you, from the streight paths of virtue,
Into the maze of Love.

DEMETRIUS
I see compassion in thy eye, that chides me,
If I have either soul, but what's contain'd
Within these words, or if one syllable
Of their full force, be not made good by me,
May all relenting thoughts in you take end,
And thy disdain be doubled, from thy pardon,
I'll count my Coronation; and that hour
Fix with a rubrick in my Calendar,
As an auspicious time, to entertain
Affairs of weight with Princes; think who now
Intreats thy mercy, come, thou sha't be kind,
And divide Titles with me.

POLIDORA
Hear me, Sir,
I lov'd you once for virtue, and have not
A thought so much unguarded, as to be won
From my truth, and innocence with any
Motives of state to affect you,
Your bright temptation mourns while it stayes here;
Nor can the triumph of glory, which made you
Forget me, so court my opinion back,
Were you no King, I should be sooner drawn
Again to love you, but 'tis now too late,
A low obedience shall become me best:
May all the joyes I want
Still wait on you, if time hereafter tell you,
That sorrow for your fault hath struck me dead,
May one soft tear drop from your eye, in pitty
Bedew my hearse, and I shall sleep securely:
I have but one word more for goodness sake,
For your own honor, Sir, correct your passion,
To her you shall love next, and I forgive you.

[Exit.

DEMETRIUS
Her heart is frozen up, nor can warm prayers
Thaw it to any softness.

PHILOCLES
I'll fetch her, Sir, again.

DEMETRIUS
Perswade her not.

PHILOCLES

You give your passion too much leave to triumph.
Seek in another what she denies.

[Enter **MACARIUS**.

MACARIUS
Where's the King? oh, Sir, you are undone,
A dangerous treason is a foot.

DEMETRIUS
What Treason?

MACARIUS
Cassander, and Eubulus have proclaim'd
Another King, whom they pretend to be
Leonatus your elder Brother, he that was,
But this morning prisoner in the Castle.

DEMETRIUS
Ha?

MACARIUS
The easie Epirotes
Gather in multitudes to advance his Title,
They have seised upon the Court, secure your person,
Whilst we raise power to curbe this Insurrection.

ANTIGONUS
Lose no time then.

DEMETRIUS
We will not Arme one Man,
Speak it agen, have I a brother living?
And must be no King.

MACARIUS
What means your Grace?

DEMETRIUS
This newes doth speak me happy, it exalts
My heart, and makes me capable of more
Than twenty Kingdoms.

PHILOCLES
Will you not, Sir, stand
Upon your guard?

DEMETRIUS

I'll stand upon my honor,
Mercy relieves me.

LISANDER
Will you lose the Kingdom?

DEMETRIUS
The World's too poor to bribe me: leave
Me all, lest you extenuate my fame, and I
Be thought to have redeem'd it by your counsel,
You shall not share one scruple in the honor;
Titles may set a gloss upon our Name,
But Virtue onely is the soul of Fame.

MACARIUS
He's strangely possest Gentlemen.

[Exeunt **OMNES**.

ACTUS QUINTUS

SCÆNA PRIMA

Enter **PHILOCLES**, and **LISANDER**.

PHILOCLES
Heres a strange turne, Lisander.

LISANDER
'Tis a Kingdom
Easily purchas'd, who will trust the faith
Of multitudes?

PHILOCLES
It was his fault, that would
So tamely give his Title to their Mercy,
The new King has possession.

LISANDER
And is like
To keep't, we are alone, what dost think of
This innovation? Is't not a fine Jigge?
A precious cunning in the late Protector
To shuffle a new Prince into the state.

PHILOCLES

I know not how they have shuffled, but my head on't,
A false card is turn'd up trump, but fates look to't.

[Enter **CASSANDER** and **EUBULUS**.

EUBULUS
Does he not carry it bravely?

CASSANDER
Excellently.
Philocles, Lisander.

PHILOCLES
LISIMACHUS
Your Lordships servants,
Are we not bound to heaven, for multiplying
These blessings on the Kingdom.

PHILOCLES
Heaven alone
Works miracles, my Lord.

LISANDER
I think your Lordship
Had as little hope once to see these Princes
Revive.

PHILOCLES
Here we must place our thanks,
Next providence, for preserving
So dear a pledge.

[Enter **LEONATUS** attended.

EUBULUS
The King.

LEONATUS
It is our pleasure
The number of our guard be doubled, give
A Largess to the Soldiers; but dismiss not
The Troops till we command.

CASSANDER
May it please.

LEONATUS
It will not please us otherwise, my Lord,

We have try'd your faith.

EUBULUS
Does he not speak with confidence?

LEONATUS
My Lords and Gentlemen, to whose faith we must
Owe next to Heaven our fortune, and our safety,
After a tedious eclipse, the day
Is bright, and we invested in those honors,
Our bloud, and birth did challenge.

CASSANDER
May no time
Be registred in our annals, that shall mention
One that had life to oppose your sacred person.

LEONATUS
Let them, whose Titles forg'd and flaw'd, suspect
Their states security, our right to Epire,
Heaven is oblig'd to prosper, treason has
No face so black to fright it, all my cares
Level to this, that I may worthily
Manage the province, and advance the honor
Of our dear Countrey, and be confident,
If an expence of bloud, may give addition
Of any happiness to you, I shall
Offer my heart the sacrifice, and rejoyce
To make my self a ghost, to have inscrib'd
Upon my marble, but whose cause I died for.

EUBULUS
May Heaven avert such danger.

CASSANDER
Excellent Prince,
In whom we see the Copy of his Father,
None but the Son of Theodosius,
Could have spoke thus.

LEONATUS
You are pleas'd to interpret well,
Yet give me leave to say in my own justice,
I have but exprest the promptness of my soul
To serve you all, but 'tis not empty wishes
Can satisfie our mighty charge, a weight
Would make an Atlas double, a Kings name
Doth sound harmoniously to men at distance;

And those who cannot penetrate beyond
The bark, and out-skin of a Common-wealth,
Or state, have eyes, but ravish'd with the Ceremony
That must attend a Prince, and understand not
What cares allay the glories of a Crown,
But good Kings find and feel the contrary,
You have try'd, my Lord, the burden, and can tell
It would require a Pilot of more years
To steer this Kingdom, now impos'd on me,
By justice of my birth.

CASSANDER
I wish not life,
But to partake those happy days, which must
Succeed these fair proceedings, we are blest,
But Sir, be sparing to your self, we shall
Hazard our joyes in you too soon, the burden
Of state affairs, impose upon your counsel.
'Tis fitter that we waste our lives than you,
Call age too soon upon you with the trouble,
And cares that threaten such an undertaking,
Preserve your youth.

LEONATUS
And choose you our Protector,
Is't that you would conclude my Lord? We will
Deserve our subjects faith for our own sake,
Not sit an idle gazer at the helm.

[Enter **MESSENGER**.

PHILOCLES
How observ'd you that,
Mark how Cassander's Planet struck.

EUBULUS
He might have look'd more calmly for all that,
I begin to fear; but do not yet seem troubled.

LEONATUS
With what news travels his haste? I must secure
My self betimes, not be a King in jest,
And wear my Crown a Tenant to their breath.

CASSANDER
 Demetrius, Sir, your brother,
With other Traitors that oppose your claims,
Are fled to the Castle of Nestorius,

And fortifie.

MESSENGER
I said not so my Lord.

CASSANDER
I'll have it thought so, hence.

[Exit **MESSEN.**

LEONATUS
Plant forces to batter
The walls, and in their ruin bring us word
They live not.

EUBULUS
Good Sir hear me.

CASSANDER
Let it work,
Were Demetrius dead, we easily might uncrown
This swoln Impostor, and my Son be fair
To piece with young Sophia, who I hear
Repents her late affront.

EUBULUS
Their lives may do
You service, let not blood stain your beginnings
The people not yet warm in their allegeance,
May think it worth their tumult to revenge it
With hazard of your self.

LEONATUS
Who dares but think it?
Yet offer first our mercy, if they yield,
Demetrius must not live, my Lord your counsel,
What if he were in heaven?

CASSANDER
You have my consent,
You sha'not stay long after him.

LEONATUS
Sophia is
Not my Sister,
To prevent all that may indanger us, we'll marry her;
That done, no matter though we stand discover'd,
For in her Title then we are King of Epire,

Without dispute.

CASSANDER
Hum; in my judgement, Sir,
That wonot do so well.

LEONATUS
What's your opinion?

CASSANDER
He countermines my plot: are you so cunning.

LEONATUS
What's that you mutter; Sir?

CASSANDER
I mutter, Sir?

LEONATUS
Best say I am no King, but some impostor
Rais'd up to gull the state.

CASSANDER
Very fine to have said within
Few hours you'd been no King, nor like to be,
Was not in the compass of High Treason
I take it.

EUBULUS
Restrein your anger, the Kings mov'd, speak not.

CASSANDER
I will speak louder, do I not know him?
That self-same hand that rais'd him to the throne
Shall pluck him from it, is this my reward?

LEONATUS
Our guard, to prison with him.

CASSANDER
Me to prison?

LEONATUS
Off with his head.

CASSANDER
My head?

EUBULUS
Vouchsafe to hear me, great Sir.

CASSANDER
How dares he be so insolent?
I ha' wrought my self into a fine condition,
Do'e know me Gentlemen?

PHILOCLES
Very well my Lord;
How are we bound to heaven for multiplying
These blessings on the Kingdom.

LEONATUS
We allow it.

EUBULUS
Counsel did never blast a Princes ear.

LEONATUS
Convey him to the sanctuary of Rebels,
Nestorius house, where our proud brother has
Enscons'd himself, they'll entertain him lovingly,
He will be a good addition to the Traitors,
Obey me, or you dye for't, what are Kings
When subjects dare affront 'em?

CASSANDER
I shall vex
Thy soul for this.

LEONATUS
Away with him: when Kings
Frown, let offenders tremble, this flows not
From any cruelty in my nature, but
The fate of an Usurper: he that will
Be confirm'd great without just title to't,
Must lose compassion, know what's good, not do't.

[Exeunt.

[Enter **POLIDORA** and her **SERVANT**.

SERVANT
Madam, the Princess Sophia.

POLIDORA
I attend her Highness.

[Enter **SOPHIA**.

How much your grace honors your humble servant.

SOPHIA
I hope my brother's well.

POLIDORA
I hope so too, Madam.

SOPHIA
Do you but hope? he came to be your guest.

POLIDORA
We are all his, whilst he is pleas'd to honor
This poor roof with his royal presence, Madam.

SOPHIA
I came to ask your pardon Polidora.

POLIDORA
You never, Madam, trespass'd upon me,
Wrong not your goodness.

SOPHIA
I can be but penitent,
Unless you point me out some other way
To satisfie.

POLIDORA
Dear Madam, do not mock me.

SOPHIA
There is no injury like that to love,
I find it now in my own sufferings:
But though I would have rob'd thee of Arcadius
Heaven knew a way to reconcile your hearts,
And punishd me in those joys you have found:
I read the story of my loss of honor,
Yet can rejoyce, and heartily, that you
Have met your own agen.

POLIDORA
Whom do you mean?

SOPHIA
My brother.

POLIDORA
He is found to himself and honor,
He is my King, and though I must acknowledge
He was the glory of my thoughts, and I
Lov'd him, as you did, Madam, with desire
To be made his, reason, and duty since,
Form'd me to other knowledge, and I now
Look on him without any wish of more
Than to be call'd his subject.

SOPHIA
Has he made
Himself less capable by being King?

POLIDORA
Of what?

SOPHIA
Of your affection.

POLIDORA
With your pardon, Madam.
Love in that sense you mean, left Polidora
When he forsook Arcadius, I disclaim
All ties between us, more than what a name
Of King must challenge from my obedience.

SOPHIA
This does confirm my jealousie, my heart,
For my sake, Madam, has he lost his value?

POLIDORA
Let me beseech your grace, I may have leave
To answer in some other cause, or person:
This argument but opens a sad wound
To make it bleed afresh; we may change this
Discourse: I would elect some subject, whose
Praises may more delight your ear than this
Can mine; let's talk of young Lisimachus.

SOPHIA
Ha? my presaging fears.

POLIDORA
How does your grace?

SOPHIA

Well, you were talking of Lisimachus,
Pray give me your opinion of him.

POLIDORA
Mine?
It will be much short of his worth: I think him
A gentleman so perfect in all goodness,
That if there be one in the world deserves
The best of women, heaven created him,
To make her happy.

SOPHIA
You have, in a little, Madam,
Exprest a volume of mankind, a miracle;
But all have not the same degree of faith,
He is but young.

POLIDORA
What Mistriss would desire
Her servant old? he has both Spring to please
Her eye and Summer to return a harvest.

SOPHIA
He is black.

POLIDORA
He sets a beauty off more rich,
And she that's fair will love him; faint complexions
Betray effeminate minds, and love of change:
Two beauties in a bed, compound few men;
He's not so fair to counterfeit a woman,
Nor yet so black, but blushes may betray
His modesty.

SOPHIA
His proportion exceeds not.

POLIDORA
That praises him, and a well compacted frame
Speaks temper, and sweet flow of elements:
Vast buildings are more oft for shew than use:
I would not have my eyes put to the travel
Of many acres, e'r I could examine
A man from head to foot; he has no great,
But he may boast, an elegant composition.

SOPHIA
I'll hear no more, you have so far out-done

My injuries to you, that I call back
My penitence, and must tell Polidora,
This revenge ill becomes her. Am I thought
So lost in soul to hear, and forgive this?
In what shade do I live? or shall I think
I have not, at the lowest, enough merit,
Setting aside my birth, to poize with yours:
Forgive my modest thoughts, if I rise up
In my own defence, and tell this unjust Lady
So great a winter hath not frozen yet
My cheek, but there is something nature planted,
That carries as much bloom, and spring upon't,
As yours. What flame is in your eye, but may
Find competition here? (forgive agen
My Virgin honor,) what is in your lip
To tice the enamour'd soul, to dwell with more
Ambition, than the yet unwither'd blush
That speaks the innocence of mine?

[Enter **DEMETRIUS**.

Oh brother?

DEMETRIUS
I'll talk with you anon, my Polidora,
Allow thy patience till my breath recover,
Which now comes laden with the richest news
Thy ear was ever blest with.

SOPHIA
Both your looks,
And voice express some welcome accident.

DEMETRIUS
Guess what in wish could make me fortunate
And heaven hath dropt that on Demetrius.

SOPHIA
What means this extasie?

DEMETRIUS
'Twere sin to busie
Thy thoughts upon't, I'll tell thee that I could
Retein some part; 'tis too wide a joy
To be exprest so soon, and yet it falls
In a few syllables, thou wot scarce believe me,
I am no King.

SOPHIA
How's that!

POLIDORA
Good Heaven forbid.

DEMETRIUS
Forbid? Heaven has reliev'd me with a mercy
I knew not how to ask, I have, they say,
An elder brother living, crown'd already,
I only keep my name Demetrius,
Without desire of more addition,
Than to return thy servant.

POLIDORA
You amaze me,
Can you rejoyce to be deposed:

DEMETRIUS
It but
Translates me to a fairer and better Kingdom
In Polidora.

POLIDORA
Me?

DEMETRIUS
Did you not say,
Were I no King, you could be drawn to love
Me agen, that was consented to in Heaven:
A Kingdom first betraid my ambitious soul
To forget thee, that, and the flattering glories,
How willingly Demetrius does resign,
The Angels know: thus naked without Titles
I throw me on thy charity, and shall
Boast greater Empire to be thine agen, than
To wear the triumphs of the world upon me.

[Enter **MACARIUS**.

MACARIUS
Be not so careless of your self, the people
Gather in multitudes to your protection
Offering their lives and fortunes, if they may
But see you Sir, and hear you speak to 'em,
Accept their duties, and in time prevent
Your ruin.

SOPHIA
Be not desperate, 'tis counsel.

DEMETRIUS
You trouble me with noise, speak Polidora.

POLIDORA
For your own sake preserve your self,
My fears distract my reason.

[Enter **ANTIGONUS**.

ANTIGONUS
Lord Lisimachus,
With something that concerns your safety, is
Fled hither, and desires a present hearing.

MACARIUS
His soul is honest, be not, Sir, a mad man,
And for a Lady, give up all our freedoms.

[Exit.

POLIDORA
I'll say any thing here, Lisimachus.

SOPHIA
Dear brother hear him.

[Enter **LISIMACHUS**.

LISIMACHUS
Sir, I come to yield
My self your prisoner, if my father have
Rais'd an Impostor to supplant your Title
Which I suspect, and inwardly do bleed for,
I shall not only, by the tender of
My self, declare my innocence, but either,
By my unworthy life, secure your person,
Or by what death you shall impose, reward
The unexpected Treason.

SOPHIA
Brave young man,
Did you not hear him Brother?

LISIMACHUS
I am not minded.

POLIDORA
Be witness Madam, I resign my heart
It never was anothers, you declare
Too great a satisfaction, I hope
This will destroy your jealousie,
Remember now your danger.

DEMETRIUS
I despise it,
What fate dares injure me?

LISIMACHUS
Yet hear me Sir.

SOPHIA
Forgive me Polidora, you are happy,
My hopes are remov'd farther, I had thought
Lisimachus had meant you for his Mistriss,
'Tis misery to feed, and not know where
To place my jealousie.

[Enter **MACARIUS**.

MACARIUS
Now 'tis too late,
You may be deafe, until the Cannon make,
You find your sense, we are shut up now by
A troop of Horse, thank your self.

POLIDORA
They will
Admit conditions.

SOPHIA
And allow us quarter.

[A **SHOUT** within.

POLIDORA
We are all lost.

DEMETRIUS
Be comforted.

[Enter **ANTIGONUS**.

ANTIGONUS

News my Lord Cassander sent by the new King.
To bear us company.

DEMETRIUS
Not as prisoner?

ANTIGONUS
It does appear no otherwise, the soldiers
Declare how much they love him, by their noise
Of scorn, and joy to see him so rewarded.

DEMETRIUS
It cannot be.

ANTIGONUS
You'll find it presently,
He curses the new King, talks treason 'gainst him
As nimble as he were in's shirt, he's here.

[Enter **CASSANDER**.

CASSANDER
Oh let me beg untill my knees take root
I' th' earth, Sir, can you pardon me?

DEMETRIUS
For what?

CASSANDER
For Treason, desperate, most malicious Treason:
I have undone you Sir.

DEMETRIUS
It does appear
You had a Will.

CASSANDER
I'll make you all the recompence I can,
But e'r you kill me, hear me, know the man,
Whom I to serve my unjust ends, advanc'd
To your throne, is an impostor, a mere counterfeit,
Eubulus' Son.

[Exit **ANTIGONUS**.

DEMETRIUS
It is not then our brother?

CASSANDER

An insolent usurper, proud, and bloudy;
Seleucus, is no leprosie upon me?
There is not punishment enough in nature
To quit my horrid act, I have not in
My stock of blood, to satisfie with weeping,
Nor could my soul, though melted to a flood
Within me, gush out tears to wash my stain off.

DEMETRIUS

How? an Impostor, what will become on's now?
We are at his mercy.

CASSANDER

Sir, the peoples hearts
Will come to their own dwelling, when they see
I dare accuse my self, and suffer for it,
Have courage then young King, thy fate cannot
Be long compell'd.

DEMETRIUS

Rise, our misfortune
Carries this good, although it lose our hopes,
It makes you friend with virtue, we'll expect
What providence will do.

CASSANDER

You are too merciful.

LISIMACHUS

Our duties shall beg heaven still to preserve you.

[Enter **ANTIGONUS**.

ANTIGONUS

Our enemy desires some parley, Sir.

LISIMACHUS

'Tis not amiss to hear their proposition.

POLIDORA

I'll wait upon you.

DEMETRIUS

Thou art my Angel, and canst best instruct me,
Boldly present our selves, you'll with Cassander.

CASSANDER

And in death be blest
To find our charity.

[Exit.

SOPHIA
Lisimachus.

LISIMACHUS
Madam.

SOPHIA
They will not miss your presence, the small time
Is spent in asking of a question.

LISIMACHUS
I wait your pleasure.

SOPHIA
Sir, I have a suit to you.

LISIMACHUS
To me? it must be granted.

SOPHIA
If you have
Cancell'd your kind opinion of me,
Deny me not to know, who hath succeeded
Sophia in your heart, I beg the name
Of your new Mistriss.

LISIMACHUS
You shall know her, Madam,
If but these tumults cease, and fate allow us
To see the Court agen, I hope you'll bring
No mutiny against her, but this is
No time to talk of Love, let me attend you.

SOPHIA
I must expect, till you are pleas'd to satisfie
My poor request, conduct me at your pleasure.

[Exeunt.

[Enter **LEONATUS, EUBULUS, BISHOP, LISANDER,** and **PHILOCLES.**

LEONATUS
They are too slow, dispatch new messengers,

To intreat 'em fairly hither, I am extasi'd,
Were you witness for me too? is it possible
I am what this affirms, true Leonatus,
And were you not my Father, was I given
In trust to you an Infant?

EUBULUS
'Tis a truth,
Our soul's bound to acknowledge, you supply'd
The absence and opinion of my Son.
Who died, but to make you my greater care
I know not of Demetrius, but suppos'd
Him dead indeed, as Epire thought you were,
Your Fathers character doth want no testimony,
Which but compar'd with what concerns Demetrius
Will prove it self King Theodosius act,
Your Royal Father.

BISHOP
I am subscrib'd to both his Legacies
By oath oblig'd to secresie, until
Thus fairly summon'd to reveal the trust.

EUBULUS
Cassander had no thought you would prove thus,
To whose policie I gave this aim, although
He wrought you up to serve but as his Engine
To batter young Demetrius, for it was
Your Fathers prudent jealousie, that made him
Give out your early deaths, as if his soul
Prophecy'd his own first, and fear'd to leave
Either of you, to the unsafe protection,
Of one, whose study would be to supplant
Your right, and make himself the King of Epire.

BISHOP
Your Sister, fair Sophia, in your Fathers
Life, was design'd to marry with Lisimachus
That guarded her; although she us'd some Art
To quit her pupillage, and being absolute,
Declar'd love to Demetrius, which enforc'd
Macarius to discover first your brother.

LEONATUS
No more, lest you destroy agen Leonatus
With wonder of his fate, are they not come yet?
Something it was, I felt within my envy
Of young Demetrius's fortune, there were seeds

Scattered upon my heart, that made it swell
With thought of Empire, Princes I see cannot
Be totally eclips'd, but wherefore stays
Demetrius and Sophia, at whose names
A gentle spirit walk'd upon my blood.

[Enter **DEMETRIUS**, **POLIDORA**, **SOPHIA**, **MACARIUS**, **CASSANDER**, **LISIMA**.

EUBULUS
They are here.

LEONATUS
Then thus I flie into their bosoms,
Nature has rectifi'd in me, Demetrius,
The wandrings of ambition, our dear Sister
You are amaz'd, I did expect it, read
Assurance there, the day is big with wonder.

MACARIUS
What means all this?

LEONATUS
Lisimachus, be dear to us,
Cassander, you are welcome too.

CASSANDER
Not I,
I do not look for't, all this sha'not bribe
My conscience to your faction, and make
Me false agen, Seleucus is no son
Of Theodosius, my dear Countrey-men
Correct your erring duties, and to that,
Your lawful King, prostrate your selves, Demetrius
Doth challenge all your knees.

DEMETRIUS
All Love and Duty,
Flow from me to my Royal King, and Brother
I am confirm'd.

CASSANDER
You are too credulous,
What can betray your faith so much?

LEONATUS
Sophia, you appear sad, as if your Will
Gave no consent to this days happiness.

SOPHIA
No joy exceeds Sophia's for your self.

LISIMACHUS
With your pardon, Sir, I apprehend
A cause that makes her troubled, she desires
To know, what other Mistriss, since her late
Unkindness I have chosen to direct
My faith and service.

LEONATUS
Another Mistriss?

LISIMACHUS
Yes, Sir.

LEONATUS
And does our Sister love Lisimachus?

SOPHIA
Here's something would confess.

LEONATUS
He must not dare
To affront Sophia.

CASSANDER
How my shame confounds me,
I beg your justice, without pity on
My age.

LEONATUS
Your pennance shall be, to be faithful
To our state hereafter,

OMNES
May you live long and happy,
Leonatus, King of Epire.

LEONATUS
But where's your other Mistriss?

LISIMACHUS
Even here, Sir.

LEONATUS
Our Sister? is this another Mistriss, Sir?

LISIMACHUS
It holds
To prove my thoughts were so when she began
Her sorrow for neglecting me, that sweetness
Deserv'd, I should esteem her another Mistriss,
Then when she cruelly forsook Lisimachus,
Your pardon Madam, and receive a heart
Proud with my first devotions to serve you.

SOPHIA
In this I am crown'd agen, now mine for ever.

LEONATUS
You have deceiv'd her happily,
Joy to you both.

DEMETRIUS
We are ripe for the same wishes,
Polidora's part of me.

POLIDORA
He all my blessing.

LEONATUS
Heaven pour full joys upon you.

MACARIUS
We are all blest,
There wants but one to fill your arms.

LEONATUS
My Mistriss,
And Wife shall be my Countrey, to which I
Was in my birth contracted, your love since
Hath plaid the Priest to perfect what was ceremony
Though Kingdoms by just Titles prove our own,
The subjects hearts do best secure a Crown.

[Exeunt **OMNES**.

EPILOGUE

There is no Coronation to day,
Unless your gentle votes do crown our Play,
If smiles appear within each Ladies eye,
Which are the leading Stars in this fair skie,

Our solemn day sets glorious, for then
We hope by their soft influence, the men
Will grace what they first shin'd on, make't appear,
(Both) how we please, and bless our covetous ear
With your applause, more welcome than the Bells
Upon a triumph, Bonfires, or what else
Can speak a Coronation. And though I
Were late depos'd, and spoil'd of Majesty,
By the kind aid of your hands, Gentlemen,
I quickly may be Crown'd a Queen agen.

JAMES SHIRLEY – A SHORT BIOGRAPHY

James Shirley was born in London in September 1596.

His education was through a collection of England's finest establishments: Merchant Taylors' School, London, St John's College, Oxford, and St Catharine's College, Cambridge, where he took his B.A. degree in approximately 1618.

He first published in 1618, a poem entitled Echo, or the Unfortunate Lovers.

As with many artists of this period full details of his life and career are not recorded. Sources say that after graduating he became "a minister of God's word in or near St Albans." A conversion to the Catholic faith enabled him to become master of St Albans School from 1623–25.

He wrote his first play, Love Tricks, or the School of Complement, which was licensed on February 10th, 1625. From the given date it would seem he wrote this whilst at St Albans but, after its production, he moved to London and to live in Gray's Inn.

For the next two decades, he would write prolifically and with great quality, across a spectrum of thirty plays; through tragedies and comedies to tragicomedies as well as several books of poetry. Unfortunately, his talents were left to wither when Parliament passed the Puritan edict in 1642, forbidding all stage plays and closing the theatres.

Most of his early plays were performed by Queen Henrietta's Men, the acting company for which Shirley was engaged as house dramatist.

Shirley's sympathies lay with the King in battles with Parliament and he received marks of special favor from the Queen.

He made a bitter attack on William Prynne, who had attacked the stage in Histriomastix, and, when in 1634 a special masque was presented at Whitehall by the gentlemen of the Inns of Court as a practical reply to Prynne, Shirley wrote the text—The Triumph of Peace.

Shirley spent the years 1636 to 1640 in Ireland, under the patronage of the Earl of Kildare. Several of his plays were produced by his friend John Ogilby in Dublin in the first ever constructed Irish theatre; The

Werburgh Street Theatre. During his years in Dublin he wrote The Doubtful Heir, The Royal Master, The Constant Maid, and St. Patrick for Ireland.

In his absence from London, Queen Henrietta's Men sold off a dozen of his plays to the stationers, who naturally, enough published them. When Shirley returned to London in 1640, he finished with the Queen Henrietta's company and his final plays in London were acted by the King's Men.

On the outbreak of the English Civil War Shirley served with the Earl of Newcastle. However when the King's fortunes began to decline he returned to London. There his friend Thomas Stanley gave him help and thereafter Shirley supported himself in the main by teaching and publishing some educational works under the Commonwealth. In addition to these he published during the period of dramatic eclipse four small volumes of poems and plays, in 1646, 1653, 1655, and 1659.

It is said that he was "a drudge" for John Ogilby in his translations of Homer's Iliad and the Odyssey, and survived into the reign of Charles II, but, though some of his comedies were revived, his days as a playwright were over.

His death, at age seventy, along with that of his wife, in 1666, is described as one of fright and exposure due to the Great Fire of London which had raged through parts of London from September 2nd to the 5th.

He was buried at St Giles in the Fields, in London, on October 29th, 1666.

JAMES SHIRLEY – A CONCISE BIBLIOGRAPHY

The following includes years of first publication, and of performance if known, together with dates of licensing by the Master of the Revels if available.

TRAGEDIES
The Maid's Revenge (licensed 9th February 1626; printed, 1639)
The Traitor (licensed 4th May 1631; printed, 1635)
Love's Cruelty (licensed 14th November 1631; printed, 1640)
The Politician (acted, 1639; printed, 1655)
The Cardinal (licensed 25th May 1641; printed, 1652).

TRAGI-COMEDIES
The Grateful Servant (licensed 3rd November 1629 as The Faithful Servant; printed 1630)
The Young Admiral (licensed 3rd July 1633; printed 1637)
The Coronation (licensed 6th February 1635, as Shirley's, but printed in 1640 as a work of John Fletcher)
The Duke's Mistress (licensed 18th January 1636; printed 1638)
The Gentleman of Venice (licensed 30th October 1639; printed 1655)
The Doubtful Heir (printed 1652), licensed as Rosania, or Love's Victory in 1640
The Imposture (licensed 10th November 1640; printed 1652)
The Court Secret (printed 1653).

COMEDIES
Love Tricks, or the School of Complement (licensed 10th February 1625; printed under its subtitle, 1631)
The Wedding (ca. 1626; printed 1629)

The Brothers (licensed 4th November 1626; printed 1652)
The Witty Fair One (licensed 3rd October 1628; printed 1633)
The Humorous Courtier (licensed 17th May 1631; printed 1640).
The Changes, or Love in a Maze (licensed 10th January 1632; printed 1639)
Hyde Park (licensed 20th April 1632; printed 1637)
The Ball (licensed 16th November 1632; printed 1639)
The Bird in a Cage, or The Beauties (licensed 21st January 1633; printed 1633)
The Gamester (licensed 11th November 1633; printed 1637)
The Example (licensed 24th June 1634; printed 1637)
The Opportunity (licensed 29th November 1634; printed 1640)
The Lady of Pleasure (licensed 15th October 1635; printed 1637)
The Royal Master (acted and printed 1638)
The Constant Maid, or Love Will Find Out the Way (printed 1640)
The Sisters (licensed 26th April 1642; printed 1653).
Honoria and Mammon (printed 1659)

DRAMAS
A Contention for Honor and Riches (printed 1633), morality play
The Triumph of Peace (licensed 3rd February 1634; printed 1634), masque
The Arcadia (printed 1640), pastoral tragicomedy
St. Patrick for Ireland (printed 1640), neo-miracle play
The Triumph of Beauty (ca. 1640; printed 1646), masque
The Contention of Ajax and Ulysses (printed 1659), entertainment
Cupid and Death (performed 26th March 1653; printed 1659), masque